SIDE-YARD SUPERHERO HONORS

University of Arkansas at Morrilton - ***One Book One Community Reading Selection***

Kent State University at Tuscarawas - ***One Book One Community Reading Selection***

Readers' Favorites - ***Silver Award, Non-Fiction Memoir***

Dan Poynter's Global eBook Award - ***Bronze***

Conversations Book Club - ***Top 12 Choice***

Cyrus Webb's - ***"25 Books Every Man Should Read"***

The Great Southeast Book Festival - ***Biography/Autobiography Honorable Mention***

Reader Views Regional Great Lakes - ***Reviewers Choice Award Winner***

New York Book Festival - ***Honorable Mention***

Eric Hoffer Award - ***Finalist***

The Great Northwest Book Festival - ***Biography/Autobiography Honorable Mention***

National Indie Excellence Award - ***Regional Non-Fiction Finalist***

The Great Southwest Book Festival - ***Biography/Autobiography Honorable Mention***

New Mexico-Arizona Book Award - ***Biography Finalist***

Royal Dragonfly Book Award - ***Newbie Non-Fiction Honorable Mention***

Royal Dragonfly Book Award - ***Biography/Memoir Honorable Mention***

HERE'S WHAT FOLKS ARE SAYING ABOUT SIDE-YARD SUPERHERO

"*Side-Yard Superhero* illustrates how we unexpectedly discover heroic qualities in our most ordinary daily acquaintances."

—Dale Bumpers
U.S. Senator from Arkansas (1975–1999)
Author of *The Best Lawyer in a One-Lawyer Town*

"You will laugh, you will cry, you will remember, and you will thank Rick Niece for re-opening a window to your childhood."

—E. Kearney Dietz
President Emeritus, Arkansas Independent Colleges and Universities

"*Side-Yard Superhero* floats back to an age of innocence and simplicity, nostalgically remembering a treasured friendship between two very different boys. A delightful read!"

—Nancy Dane
Author of *The Tattered Glory Series*

"Rick Niece vividly describes the charms of small-town America, where neighborly friendships develop character, attitude, and our responsibility to others."

—Dr. David L. Warren, President
National Association of Independent Colleges and Universities

"Welcome to DeGraff, Ohio. I promise you will enjoy the visit."

—Gary Comer
Mayor of DeGraff

"With a lyrical ability to retrieve carefully pocketed memories, Rick Niece reaches across generations to touch every heart."

—Joey Halinski
Advisory Board Member, The National Museum of Women in the Arts

"*Side-Yard Superhero* encourages us to reconnect with the unique faces and places that make childhood worth remembering."

—Steve Houchin
Rick's boyhood friend • Managing Partner, International Leadership Associates

SIDE-YARD
SUPERHERO
Life Lessons from an
Unlikely Teacher

SIDE-YARD
SUPERHERO

Life Lessons from an Unlikely Teacher

By Rick D. Niece, Ph.D.

Five Star Publications, Inc
Chandler, AZ

Linda F. Radke, President
Five Star Publications, Inc.
P.O. Box 6698
Chandler, AZ 85246-6698

www.RickNieceBooks.com

Library of Congress Cataloging-in-Publication Data

Niece, Rick D.
Side-yard superhero : life lessons from an unlikely teacher / by Rick D. Niece.
p. : ill. ; cm. -- (Fanfare for a hometown ; bk. 1)
Originally published: Austin, Tex. : Synergy Books, c2009.
ISBN-13: 978-1-58985-090-3
ISBN-10: 1-58985-090-4
eISBN: 978-1-58985-091-0
Audio Book: 978-1-58985-097-2
1. Niece, Rick D.--Childhood and youth--Anecdotes. 2. Friendship in children--
Anecdotes. 3. De Graff (Ohio)--Social life and customs--20th century. I. Title.
F496.4.N54 A3 2011
977.1/043/092   2011935239

Electronic edition provided by
www.eStarPublish.com

the eDivision of Five Star Publications, Inc.

Printed in the United States of America

Cover & Page Design: Kris Taft Miller
Chapter Design: Kris Taft Miller
Project Manager: Patti Crane

*This book is written with the intent of being as accurate as possible. It is based upon
the author's memories of events and experiences.*

For

My wife, Sherée,

my parents, Lewie and Dode,

my brothers, Jeff and Kurt,

Jay and Bonnie Parrot,

Noel, Darlene, and Devon McDowell,

Richard, Sally, and Pam Geyer,

and the citizens of DeGraff.

But most of all,

this is for Bernie.

AUTOMYTHOGRAPHY

We would expect the recounting of our lives to be works of nonfiction, and they are. Most importantly, they are *what* we think we remember and *how* we think we remember it. The things that have happened to us and the people we have known all become iridescent memories based upon the author's truth and personal narrative. Those memories are an automythography.

PROLOGUE

WHO KNOWS WHY?

Who knows why
    we remember what we remember?
    Forget what we forget?
    Keep what we keep?
Who knows why
    the sight of kids playing catch
    takes me back to an all-dirt infield
    where Little Leaguers in rubber cleats
    use wooden bats with necessary trademarks?
Who knows why
    the grease-splattered scent of chicken frying
    takes me back to my grandmother's kitchen,
    crisping legs and wings oiling paper towels
    while cooling on the countertop
    through a churchless Sunday morning?
Who knows why
    a dozen orchestrated notes from "A Summer Place"
    take me back to a high school gym dance
    and the first time a virgin velvet dress
    pressed innocently against
    my Penney's new blue blazer?

Who knows why
    the gentle petting
    of a sleek dog's slender flank
    takes me back to bicycle rides
    down rural county roads
    or along small-town sidewalks
    where anxious front porches
    await their daily newspaper?
I know why.
At birth we are divided
    into two groups
    and assigned our roles.
In one group are
    the designated memory makers.
In the other are the memory keepers,
    my favorite.
Memory keepers
always know why.

SIDE-YARD
SUPERHERO

By Rick D. Niece, Ph.D.

CHAPTER ONE

A LATE NIGHT WAKE-UP CALL

Calls past midnight are seldom good news. I tried to sound awake but managed only a not-too-convincing hello. When I heard my mother's excited voice at the other end, I immediately began running through a mental checklist of potential tragedies. She is, after all, the family's clearinghouse for death, illness, and all other things serious.

"Honey, are you awake?"

"Yeah, yeah. What happened, Mom? Is everyone all right?"

"I know where Bernie Jones is," she said, ignoring my question. "I tried to call you earlier. You sound like you were asleep. Why aren't you using the answering machine we bought you last Christmas?"

Since my parents' retirement to Arizona, my mother often forgets the time difference between there and Arkansas where we live. I touched my wife on the shoulder to let her know everything was okay, but Sherée remained asleep.

"Bernie Jones?" I whispered. "You know where Bernie is?"

"Yes, Jinny Knief telephoned me about him. He's at the Heartland Nursing Home in Lakeview. I knew you'd want to know right away."

Rick D. Niece, Ph.D.

A rapid-fire montage of childhood scenes filled my mind. Some included Bernie, while others were simply fragments of people, places, and times in DeGraff so many years ago. Once this movie of memories began, I became distracted.

"Honey," my mom interrupted, "are you still there?"

"Yes, Mom, sorry. Thanks for calling. I'll talk to you tomorrow." My mother rarely picks up on my exit lines.

"I knew you'd want to know about Bernie. Do you think you'll visit him when you're back in Ohio for the wedding? I don't believe there's anyone in Bernie's family still living, and I doubt he has any friends left."

"I'm sure you're right. Yes, I do want to see him again. As a matter of fact, I've been thinking about him a lot recently." I drifted again to the scenes that had not stopped playing through my head. I tried to slow them down but could not, and they remained just out of reach.

"Are you still there?"

"Yes, Mom, I'm still here. Listen, I'll call you tomorrow, I promise. I have a big day ahead of me and need to get back to sleep. Love you, good night."

Digital clocks are an unrelenting curse of exactness. At 3:03 a.m., I was still awake and thinking about Bernie Jones and my life growing up in DeGraff. I felt overwhelmed by the memories and by the thought of soon returning to Ohio for my cousin's wedding. I hadn't been back in years. A mixture of sadness and happiness blurred together, and I began to cry.

I kept my promise the next day and called my mother. I like keeping promises, and I assured her I'd see Bernie when I was back in Ohio. That was another promise, made a long time ago, that I wanted to keep as well.

The Ohio trip had to be brief because I needed to be back on campus by Monday evening. Sherée had a weekend fund-raising event in Little Rock and couldn't go with me. I don't like traveling alone, but knew that once I'd arrived, after managing the airports on my own, I'd be okay. My aunt and uncle in Lima had invited me to stay with them, and I was looking forward to seeing them and my cousins. I was sorry I wouldn't have time for Jinny Knief, our next-door neighbor during my years in DeGraff. She was the sweetest lady I've ever known, but seeing her would have to wait for another trip.

My flight was scheduled to land in Columbus on Friday afternoon. I'd rent a car and be in Lima in time for the evening rehearsal dinner. The wedding was Saturday. On Sunday, I'd visit Bernie in the nursing home, before returning to Arkansas on Monday. It was a quick trip planned out to the moment. Actually, it was a great plan. After more than forty years, I was going to see Bernie Jones.

CHAPTER TWO

SMALL TOWNS HAVE NO SECRETS

DeGraff, Ohio, is one of those barely visible towns people can pass through without noticing. During the ninety seconds it takes to drive from one end to the other, I imagine most say, "Who would want to live here?" I suspect some might secretly answer, "Me, maybe."

When we moved there from Oberlin, Ohio, DeGraff was a quaint little town with a population of about 900 people. My guess is that now, several decades later, it is still quaint and still one hundred short of a grand. Don't get me wrong. It's a great place. DeGraff overcompensates by being grand in other ways.

My dad attended college in Oberlin after his hitch in the Navy during World War II and, benefiting from the G.I. Bill, graduated from the Oberlin Conservatory of Music with a major in piano and minors in everything else instrumental and vocal. The offer to teach music to grades one through twelve, in a rustic one-building school district, lured him and his family to DeGraff.

Besides me, there were three others in our family—Dad, Mom, and my younger brother Jeff. The move was easy for my parents because they were both originally from that part of Ohio and anxious to return to small-town living. My brother and I didn't have a vote, but it didn't matter as towns soon become hometowns in very serendipitous ways. I was four when we moved to DeGraff. My youngest brother, Kurt, was born after we'd lived there for five years and, by virtue of that, is the only true native.

We lived there for sixteen years but, in the minds of most townspeople, we were forever "new to the area." If you were not born, raised, and predicted to die in DeGraff, you were eternally a newcomer. Since we eventually moved away, I guess they were right. By their standards, we were short-termers.

By any measure, I was a typical kid in a typical small town (that is, if you can stay typical while your father is the school's only music teacher and the superintendent lives across the street). In many ways, I felt as though I were a specimen under the microscope. You know, in the "don't embarrass your father in front of the superintendent or the other teachers" kind of way. I think my parents would agree I was pretty good, usually listened, and managed to avoid serious trouble.

A newspaper route was the first true love of my life. With my faithful Dalmatian Lady gliding stride by stride next to my bright red, twenty-four-inch Huffy, I raced the streets and sidewalks of DeGraff perfectly pitching hand-rolled papers onto my customers' front porches. If delivering newspapers were an Olympic event, I'm pretty sure I could have qualified as DeGraff's first medal recipient (with Lady sharing the platform with me, of course).

Life in DeGraff was as perfect as any boy could ask for—and DeGraff was also home to Bernie Jones.

I took over Billy Neal's paper route when I was nine. Billy lived a street over from us and was one of the big guys I admired, but he never cared much for me. I was dependable and eager to start a career, while Billy was quasi-dependable at best and eager to get out of his.

His last day as a paperboy was on a Saturday, and he finally took me with him door-to-door as he collected thirty cents for the week of daily newspapers. Later that afternoon, I bicycled along with him as he delivered the papers, but by Monday I would be on my own.

At our first collection stop, Bob and Janet Hall's house, Billy rang the doorbell several times and even knocked on the door, but no one answered. Wanting to be helpful, I went over to one of the front windows and peeked inside, trying to see if anyone was hiding behind a sofa or a lamp. That happened in our house if either of my parents was avoiding someone at the door. The next thing I knew, Billy cracked me on the side of the head and hollered, "What are you doing, you little jerk? Never peep into a customer's window! Do you want to get us arrested or something?"

Of course I didn't want to get arrested, and who knew what Billy's unspecified "something" might involve? I'm forever thankful to him for saving me from a life of crime as a peeping Rickie. I never looked into another customer's window.

As we rode along, Billy told me that most of the customers were fairly normal, at least by DeGraff standards, except for three. He warned me that Fern Burdette was a crazy old lady who'd talk your leg off if you let her. Laughing, he added that was probably how she'd lost hers. Then, shaking his head like someone who'd heard about the sad details of her life more than once but still didn't care, he smirked as he told me Miss Lizzie Moore was a reclusive spinster who might as well have been a hermit. Finally, in a loud whisper, Billie said Bernie Jones was also on the route and declared that was all he was going to tell me.

It didn't matter. I thought I already knew all there was to know about the three of them, especially Bernie Jones. Even little kids quickly learn that small towns have no secrets and little hesitation in sharing them.

DeGraff was divided into four zones for newspaper delivery and, as far as I was concerned, I had the choicest route and the best customers. Four of us delivered *The Bellefontaine Examiner*, a daily paper except for Sunday published in Bellefontaine, the county seat and largest city in Logan County. All four of us—John Slater and the Tamplin brothers, Charles and Herb—kept our routes for a long time. Other kids in DeGraff wanted our jobs, but we were not about to give them up. We knew we had a good thing. I had my route from the time I was nine until I graduated from high school. The others kept theirs for almost as long. We made ten cents a week per customer, and with my seventy-two customers the pay was good.

The newspapers were brought to DeGraff in a tired-looking Chevrolet pickup truck driven by a questionable character named Senior Junior. I swear that was his name. After Senior Junior delivered the two large bundles to the detached garage at Art Haugen's house, we'd count out the papers we needed for our individual routes and talk "man talk" while folding the papers tightly for throwing onto porches. Senior Junior sometimes hung around to tell us about an older woman he was dating or what he'd already read in the paper during his trip to DeGraff, proud of his ability to drive and read at the same time.

I always liked Senior Junior, although I thought his unusual name was oxymoronic, kind of like delicious liver. You see, Senior Junior was a sophomore when he dropped out of high school. Try to figure that one out. I wish I'd asked him about his name and how he got it, but I never did. During my freshman year in high school, he was killed in an accident while driving our papers from Bellefontaine. A bulk milk truck pulled out in front of him. My guess is he was engrossed in reading the daily news and forgot to look up. The next day, Senior Junior made the front page of *The Bellefontaine Examiner*, and in adolescent logic we thought it was pretty ironic he couldn't read about himself. In that story we also learned his real name was Milburn.

I'd sling the canvas bag of seventy-two folded newspapers over my shoulder and head off on my bicycle. I became expert at riding fast and flinging the papers perfectly onto each porch as I sped by. I developed a technique of leading porches better than a champion skeet shooter leads clay pigeons. Up and down hills, around sharp corners, within narrow alleyways, and through the center of town, I raced and threw, threw and raced. Most days, my route took about an hour-and-a-half, starting around 4:00 p.m.

My customers knew I was approaching because I loved to whistle—loudly. No one seemed annoyed by it, as far as I know. Because of my musical upbringing, I usually whistled something classical. Beethoven, Tchaikovsky, and Rachmaninoff were standards in my repertoire, but every now and then the latest Elvis Presley, Everly Brothers, Lesley Gore, or Kingston Trio tune caught my fancy, and I'd add it to my list.

I remember riding in the backseat of a car with my Uncle Robert and Aunt LaVelva when I was about four or five. Uncle Robert asked what I wanted to be when I grew up.

He could really whistle and was able to imitate perfectly at least a dozen different birdcalls. I told him I was going to be a professional whistler and wanted to hire him to be my trainer. They both laughed, but I was serious.

Each day, I'd speed down the hill on Boggs Street, race past the box factory (offcially known as The Mid-State Container Corporation, and DeGraff's only major industry) and prepare for the bumps of the railroad tracks that ran through the middle of town. I'd start whistling a little louder, stop suddenly, and then listen for the excited voice from the side yard of the first house on the right after the tracks.

"Rickie, my boy, hurry up!" I think he waited all day every day for me to deliver the paper. I liked all of my customers, but Bernie Jones was my favorite.

Bernie's dad was a rural mail carrier and his mom was a housewife. I seldom saw either of them but occasionally, when I'd deliver the paper, Bernie's mom would be hanging laundry in the backyard. I don't remember ever seeing her smile, and I thought I knew the reason. Although Mr. Jones also seemed stoical, I did experience his anger one Saturday morning during my weekly collection for the paper. Bernie usually had the money jangling in his front shirt pocket and ready for me, but this Saturday his father made a point of paying me himself.

On holidays like Thanksgiving, Christmas, and the Fourth of July, a paper wasn't published. For those shortened weeks when the paper was delivered five days instead of six, it was only a quarter instead of the usual thirty cents. Most customers, without hesitation, would still pay me the thirty cents, and I'd carefully place the extra nickel in my left front pocket instead of slipping it into the nickel slot of the four-cylinder change maker attached to my belt. The metal changer held pennies, nickels, dimes, and quarters, and was only used for official business purposes. My left front pocket was for bonus nickels.

I looked forward to paperless holidays because, by the time I finished collecting, my pocket bulged like David Downing's cheek when he had it stuffed full with Mail Pouch chewing tobacco. David worked at the DeGraff Stockyards and Meat Packing Company where, among the cattle and pigs, chewing tobacco was considered acceptable.

Two collection Saturdays after the Fourth of July, Bernie's dad met me at the front door before I had a chance to knock.

"Here's you a quarter," he said harshly.

My voice quavered. "But, Mr. Jones, the paper's thirty cents."

"You were paid thirty cents last week when it should've only been twenty-five. No paper on the Fourth of July, remember? You owe me a nickel. Do you take advantage of all of your customers like that?"

My brain went numb. I couldn't think. I suddenly felt like one of the thieving boys working within Fagin's gang of orphans in Charles Dickens' *Oliver Twist*. They didn't know any better either, but at least I was clean, well fed, and had parents who cared about me.

"Most of my customers give me the extra nickel," I finally managed to mutter, eyes cast downward studying his shoes and mine. "I think they want me to have it."

"Then they're damn fools." He turned and closed the door.

I didn't see Bernie that morning, and he wasn't in the side yard when I delivered the paper later in the afternoon. I spent the rest of the weekend wondering if he was being punished for my five-cent transgression.

I'd never known anyone like Bernie Jones. I was pretty

sure that my delivering the paper was the high point of his day. There were many times he was the high point of mine. I couldn't spend a lot of time with Bernie because he was toward the beginning of my route, and I had customers waiting for their papers. Six o'clock was suppertime at our house, so I had a built-in deadline. But I knew whatever time I had for him was precious and appreciated.

Bernie was born with cerebral palsy and was confined to a wheelchair.

SMALL TOWNS

Small towns are like
> an older brother,
> a favorite aunt and uncle,
> another set of parents
even when you are not orphaned.
And small towns do not mind being second.
Small towns raise you.
> They look after you.
> > They nag at you
> in a positive way.
Small towns ask for nothing in return,
> > in true unconditional love,
> when you return
no matter how many years later.
And even if you are both
> no longer what you were,
you are each as you should be
> > remembered.

13

CHAPTER THREE

BERNIE JONES

When Billy Neal told me Bernie Jones was on the paper route, I'll admit I was afraid of meeting him. Who knows why kids fear what they fear? I was curious, sure. Nonetheless, I was afraid. During Sunday supper the night before my first day to deliver papers, I asked Dad what to expect when I met Bernie. What should I say to him? How should I treat him? What could we talk about?

My dad, in logical *Father Knows Best* fashion, replied I should talk to Bernie like I talked to any of my friends. He then added, "Who knows? You may like him and become friends."

And we did become friends, even though our meeting on my first day to deliver his paper was anything but smooth. I'm still uncertain how either one of us survived that day to begin a friendship.

I stopped at the box factory parking lot, just before the railroad tracks, to catch my breath and my nerve. I could see Bernie in his wheelchair. He seemed to be looking in my direction. I couldn't tell if he saw me because his head kept rolling back and forth, and I had a hard time following his eyes. I had the feeling he somehow knew I was close by and was watching me.

After another minute, I took a deep breath and coasted down the hill and over the tracks. When he saw me, his arms and legs began windmilling frantically. I parked my bike a few feet from him in the side yard, reached for a paper, and froze. I could not move a muscle while every one of Bernie's seemed to be twitching. Bernie was fast-forwarding while I was freeze-framed. This was not going well.

Bernie said something in a halting, guttural voice. I couldn't understand him.

"What?" I stammered.

Bernie garbled again, and I continued to stammer. We were in those moments equally inarticulate. Finally, after at least half a dozen attempts, I understood his five words.

"Where's Billy? Who are you?"

"He quit! I'm Rickie! Gotta go!"

And that was it. I dropped the paper by his chair, jumped on my bike, and raced away. I don't remember delivering any of the other papers on the rest of my route, although I'm sure I did. We received only one telephone call that evening, from Jake Long—a customer I'd missed. Dad drove me to his house to deliver his paper and on the way home, I told him about meeting Bernie. I remember putting my head in Dad's lap and crying.

Dad, God bless him, simply said I'd do better the next time I saw Bernie, and he gave me wonderful advice. He said not to become fixated on my own nervousness but to focus on making Bernie feel at ease with me. He then said he was proud of me. That made me feel better even though I knew I'd done nothing to earn his pride.

The next day, I didn't stop at the box factory, but instead raced over the railroad tracks and rode straight toward Bernie. I parked my bike, walked right up to him, and placed the newspaper on his lap. "Hi, I'm Rickie."

"Well, Rickie, my boy, I'm Bernie." He only had to say it twice before I understood. I was focused.

I reached out to shake his hand the way my Grandpa Jack

had taught me with the words, "Shake hands like a man, not like a fish. Shake with a firm grasp. You can learn a lot about a man from his handshake."

But Bernie's hand was swinging around, and we never connected. I must have looked like I was swatting away a swarm of gnats. By this time, I would have settled for a fish shake.

I then asked an embarrassingly stupid question. Actually, it was a moronic and imbecilic question, the kind that hangs out there like a clothesline of irretrievable holey underwear.

"What do you like to play?"

Crap—what do you like to play? What do you like to play?

At that moment, I knew I was a simpleton, a nine-year-old half-wit who'd probably live his entire life and never be full-witted. I decided right then and there that I was quitting the route after only my second day, figuring I could still build a respectable résumé out of "Former Newspaper Boy: Two Days Experience."

Bernie laughed. For the first time, I saw his banana-skin yellow teeth. I had been warned about his teeth, and they were a sight to behold.

I laughed back. "Pretty stupid question, right?"

"Yeah, stupid question."

"What do you like, Bernie?"

"I like *Dick Tracy*."

This time I understood exactly what Bernie said, and it was at that moment our friendship began. I also liked *Dick Tracy*, cartoonist Chester Gould's ingenious creation. Our every late-afternoon newspaper delivery ritual began with me unfolding his paper and reading aloud to him the latest *Dick Tracy* comic strip. During our years of friendship, I grew into full-wittedness while reading a comic strip to a wheelchair-bound boy with cerebral palsy.

17

Except for his eyes, I don't think Bernie Jones had control over any part of his body. He was strapped into his wheelchair by a large leather belt wrapped around his middle and buckled at the back of the chair. When I'd pedal into sight, his arms would flail like the wings of a wounded turkey with legs kicking in the air, and he'd laugh a throaty laugh through his mouthful of corncob teeth.

"Rickie, my boy, where you been? What's going on with *Dick Tracy*? Is Sparkle in this one?"

Each afternoon before folding my papers in Haugen's garage, I'd quickly thumb through the pages to get to the section of black-and-white comics and *Dick Tracy*, the sixth panel down. I'd read the strip slowly for my own enlightenment and then practice it softly under my breath in preparation for reading it to Bernie. I wanted to know what words to dramatically emphasize and when to sneak in extended pauses in order to get Bernie in full whirlybird motion. After teasing him with the long pauses, I'd anxiously anticipate his reaction, and he never let me down.

"Why'd you stop? Come on, Rickie, my boy, why'd you stop? Did something bad happen?"

This was during the dreaded Flattop Jr. story line. He was as evil as his vile father, Flattop Sr. who'd menaced our hero a couple of decades earlier. Bernie and I swore that Flattop Jr. was worse than his old man.

When it came to hairstyles, flattops were popular among a lot of teenagers. There were exceptions though. DeGraff's slightly delinquent James Dean imitators—guys like Bill Greg and Ronnie Walker—set themselves apart with their pompadours and ducktails that they "varnished" to perfection with more than just a little dab of Brylcreem.

Cecil Carr, the town barber, charged one dollar for regular haircuts and $1.25 for a flattop. Bernie and I wouldn't have wanted one even if Cecil had offered to cut it for free. We wore our hair cropped short.

Bernie and I hated Flattop Jr. and cringed every time he got the better of Dick Tracy and his partner Sam Catchem. Flattop Jr. became more villainous with each reading, his mockery of our hero frustrating us both. We both shamelessly rejoiced when Flattop Jr. was killed by policewoman Lizz Groove. Bernie's exuberance quickly turned to shock, however, when we learned during the elaborate plot finale that Flattop Jr.'s last name was Jones— Flattop Jones, Jr. After I read the panel, Bernie sat almost motionless. Now, I'd never seen him motionless, but this time was pretty close. I nodded sympathetically to him, turned, and pedaled away to finish my route. We never uttered Flattop Jr.'s surname again.

I think Bernie had a crush on Sparkle Plenty, the beautifully shaped daughter of B.O. Plenty and his wife, Gravel Gertie. Whenever Sparkle appeared in one of the *Dick Tracy* strips, Bernie would ask me to re-read it while showing him the illustrations. I'd then kid him, and he'd get embarrassed with his ears turning maraschino-cherry red while denying any romantic interest. But we both knew his fantasy.

Over the years, I think I was the only other person— other than his mom and dad—who fully understood Bernie's nearly incoherent speech. His voice had a croupy, gasping quality to it. But in the same way six-year-olds understand the fractured, inarticulate language of their two-year-old siblings, I understood Bernie. After a few weeks of friendship, I understood each word and every sentence perfectly. Communication became second nature between us.

Rick D. Niece, Ph.D.

Our afternoon routine seldom varied. After I'd read
Dick Tracy, he'd ask about my day in school, wanting
to know the best thing I had learned. Bernie never went
to school. This was well before special education or
any other specialty training programs in DeGraff. So
I was the primary source of his informal education. I
think my eventual interest in teaching probably began
subconsciously with Bernie.

Because he was intrigued by science and literature,
whatever I was taking during a particular year in either
subject became his mini-curriculum. I think he liked
science because he wanted to know more about why things
are as they are. He never asked me, but I believe he was
searching for answers about himself and his condition.
Although I never heard him complain, not once in all those
years, I think he was curious to know whether he or his
parents had done something wrong. I didn't know and was
of no help in that regard.

He enjoyed *Beowulf* during my junior year in English,
and for several weeks after we finished reading it in class,
he'd ask me to retell the story about Grendel and his
mother. My Old English dialect was hardly authentic, but
Bernie enthusiastically appreciated my efforts.

I remember one spring when I was in junior high school,
Bernie shared a wish of his that stayed with me for months
after. (In truth, it has stayed with me a lifetime.) "You know
what I wish, Rickie, my boy?" he mused. I shook my head.
"I wish we had two-way wrist radios like Dick Tracy and
Sam Catchem."

Brilliant Smith, the blind son of wealthy industrialist
Diet Smith, invented the two-way wrist radio, Dick Tracy's
most famous gadget. Every kid I knew dreamed about
having one.

"With a wrist radio," he continued, "I could listen when

you're in class. I could hear everything myself."

At that moment I had a glimpse into Bernie's world and saw how hungry he was to be like other kids. He wanted to go to school and study and learn. The rest of us complained about school, but Bernie longed for it. And now I longed for it for him. Several years later, when Brilliant Smith invented the two-way wrist television, I imagined Bernie's ecstasy at the thought of us with televisions strapped to our wrists.

"Yeah, Bernie," I answered softly. "Wrist radios really would be something. Maybe someday we'll own a set."

We knew we never would, but in that moment of good friend wistfulness, his wish was hope enough for both of us. During the next couple of weeks, I listened extra carefully at school and appreciated being in class.

CHAPTER FOUR

NOTHING HIDDEN

Fern Burdette's house was a few blocks before Bernie's on my paper route. Billy Neal had made no secret of the fact that he didn't like Fern, but she fascinated me immediately. I never knew for certain if Fern thought of me as a real friend, but I'd have been honored if she did. I'm not certain what I considered her to be. I just know she was really interesting. No one in DeGraff was quite like her. Fern was the very definition of character in every sense of the word, and I still smile when I think about her.

Fern Burdette left our town to become a newspaper journalist after graduating from DeGraff High School in 1904, which sounded like ancient history to me. She traveled the world on assignments and, as a female reporter, was a trendsetter. Entering a male-dominated occupation, being single, wearing a wooden leg, and spitting like a man, Fern appeared out of place almost anywhere, but especially in DeGraff, and she seemed to relish that fact.

After retiring from the newspaper business, Fern moved back to DeGraff. She liked that I was a paperboy and said she was proud we shared the newspaper business as our profession. She talked a lot about her days as a journalist and lamented how current editors and their papers had gone soft, burying real news on the back pages and filling the front page with fluff. She'd routinely quote her first boss, the editor of a paper where she had apprenticed in Kansas City: "Fern, never hide the news from your readers. Keep it right in front of them." And that's how Fern lived her life, with nothing hidden and everything up front.

I once asked why, with all the places to choose from, she'd decided to return to DeGraff. "My life got too complicated, Rickie," she said, "and I needed to get away from that life and back to a snail's pace." She spit while chewing her ever-present wad of gum. "This is simple, and I like simple. Besides, DeGraff is about as lifeless as I could get while still breathing." I knew old Fern actually cared for DeGraff, but she never wanted anyone to know she had within her even an ounce of sentimentality.

Fern was a trendsetter in another way as well, so far ahead of her time it's difficult to calculate. Fern wore a brassiere as her normal piece of outer clothing—no blouse, no shirt, no sweater, just a brassiere from the waist up. That was Fern, with nothing hidden and everything up front. She went shopping in downtown DeGraff that way, she paraded with her dog on long walks that way, she drove her wood-paneled station wagon around town that way, and she shared a portion of her Saturday mornings with me that way. If she was a scandal, no one had the nerve to tell her.

Some might have considered her pornographic or at the very least vulgar, but I never thought of her like that. She was just Fern—brassiere wearing, hard drinking, wooden leg walking, frequent spitting, world interesting Fern.

As far as I knew, Fern had only one true love in her life and that was her well-trained, full-blooded Dalmatian named Duke, as beautiful a dog as I ever laid eyes on. My Lady, who accompanied me daily on the newspaper route, was also a Dalmatian, but she was also part Greyhound and much thinner and sleeker in the flanks than Duke.

I enjoyed stopping at Fern's house when collecting for the paper. I'd usually get there about 10:00 a.m. on Saturday. She'd be sitting in an old fabric-covered stuffed chair on her cluttered, veranda-type front porch with major city newspapers strewn around her, Duke at her feet, and an extra glass of icy lemonade waiting for me on a small bench. She'd warn me not to get our lemonade glasses mixed up because mine was the only one containing just lemonade.

The first time she made the comment and I didn't get it, she pointed to a bottle of Jack Daniels by her chair and said she could count on three things only: Duke, Jack, and me. I didn't mind being third. Our Saturday morning routines were always the same, except during the winter months when we'd have cups of hot tea instead of lemonade, again with her warning not to mix our cups.

Duke was one smart dog. I loved Lady, but she could only lift her right paw to shake hands no matter how hard I worked to train her. Fern's Duke could have starred on *The Ed Sullivan Show*. Fern would command, "Duke, how many pennies in a nickel?" Duke would reply, "Bark, bark, bark, bark, bark," and then, I swear on a Bible, the dog would smile.

"Duke, fetch me *The New York Times*." Duke would nuzzle his nose through the mound of papers surrounding Fern, paw out *The New York Times*, gently grip it in his mouth, and place it on Fern's lap.

Duke even paid me for Fern's weekly papers. "Duke, get Rickie's money," Fern would command and then sit up straight in her chair. Duke would stretch his head behind Fern's waist, grasp the envelope from Fern's back pocket, and bring it to me. Somehow, the envelope was never drooly.

After Duke's tricks, Fern would wave him back to his rug. "Lie down, honey, the adults are going to talk now." Even though I was just a kid, Fern treated me like a grown-up. But before going to his rug, Duke always trotted over

25

to Fern for an exchange. I never know how to explain the exchange without it sounding abnormal, but in all the years I knew Fern Burdette it seemed as normal as snow in January. Fern would lean down toward Duke, Duke would lift his head, and Fern would deftly transfer her wad of gum from her mouth to his. Then flopping down on the rug in the corner of the porch, butt to butt with Lady, Duke would contentedly chew "their" gum. Okay, this next part is disgusting but, after our morning talk, Fern would request the gum back, there'd be another exchange, and we'd say our good-byes. Gum must have kept its flavor longer in those days.

Much of what I know about journalism, the world, and eccentricity, I learned from Fern Burdette during our Saturday morning talks. They never lasted more than about fifteen minutes. Much like a Lowell Thomas newsreel, they were my guides to foreign adventure. Fern told tales in a *Reader's Digest* condensed style, and her journalist background made the stories interesting and to the point.

One Saturday morning, Fern met me at the sidewalk before I could walk to the porch. I knew instantly something was wrong. "Don't come on the porch, Rickie. We lost Duke last night, and I got him laid out on his rug. I'm going to bury him in the backyard, but I wanted to tell you first."

"You need any help?" I squeaked, tears cascading down my cheeks and wetting my T-shirt. "Can I help, Fern?"

"No, Rickie," she said, avoiding my gaze, "this is one thing you're too young for. I'll take care of him myself." I left Fern alone with Duke.

I never saw Fern Burdette again. She wasn't on the porch when I delivered the paper that afternoon. I heard she'd driven herself to Mary Rutan Hospital in Bellefontaine and checked herself in. Fern had never been sick a day in her life, but she told the doctor she just was not feeling right. Dad was going to drive me to visit her on Wednesday, but she died in her sleep Tuesday night.

I remember hoping heaven didn't have a dress code and allowed chewing gum and mathematical dogs.

CHAPTER FIVE

THE THATCHERVILLE HILL ADVENTURE

The boundaries of Bernie's life were extremely small. Although his house was on a street that paralleled Main Street and the center of town, he didn't have much to look at. The buildings that comprised the box factory blocked Bernie's view of downtown. The two-story Carter house, boarding Mrs. Carter and her two adult children who still lived at home, was positioned directly across the street on a yard gone to seed. That was pretty much the extent of Bernie's side-yard worldview.

Miss Lizzie Moore lived beside Bernie. A strange and intriguing spinster, Miss Lizzie, as far as anyone could determine, never left her house. Her groceries and mail were delivered outside the front door, but I never saw her walk outside to get them. On the newspaper collection days when she didn't want to be bothered, I'd find the money under the front doormat.

When she did come to the door, Miss Lizzie was always nice to me, and we'd have a conversation after she stuck her arm around the slightly opened screen door to give me the change for her weekly paper. She'd occasionally ask how the "crippled boy next door" was doing, and I'd tell

Rick D. Niece, Ph.D.

her Bernie was getting along fine, emphasizing his name. She didn't seem to catch onto my hints about that, or didn't want to, and continued to refer to him as the crippled boy. As much as I hated the term, I don't think she meant it in a disrespectful way.

Although Bernie's world was limited, he did relish two characters: Dick Tracy, of course, but also Flippo the Clown. I was able to keep him current on Dick Tracy but with Flippo the Clown, he was on his own. Flippo had a matinee movie television show for kids every weekday. His program was broadcast from a station in Columbus, so Flippo was a clown of limited celebrity. Bernie loved Flippo's corny jokes, vaudeville routines, and slapstick squirt-water-in-your-eye-from-a-fake-lapel-flower gags. The show also featured movies (usually Andy Hardy, Henry Aldrich, Shirley Temple, Tarzan, or B grade horror flicks) shown over a two- to three-day period. Bernie delighted in the movies and Flippo's high jinks.

Before our daily dose of *Dick Tracy*, Bernie would try to tell me one of Flippo's latest lame jokes. He'd usually laugh right through the punch line or just as often forget it altogether. It didn't matter though, because Bernie's joke telling was much better than the joke itself. If Flippo the Clown made Bernie feel good, then Flippo was all right by me.

Even though Bernie's world was confined, I never heard him complain, and that's why I tried to accommodate his periodic, sometimes illogical requests. Although most of his ideas defied reason, he did happen upon a plausible adventure every now and then. One time, he decided he wanted me to take him around on my route as I collected from my customers, arguing that since I knew how he spent his time, he wanted to see how I spent some of mine.

I didn't dismiss his idea right away and told Bernie I'd

30

consider it. It had possibilities, and as I thought through the logistics of having Bernie in tow, I came up with a plan. Since Bernie's house was about one-third of the way into my route, backtracking with him made no sense, so the first third was out. The last third of the route was on the other side of town and involved the murderous Harshbarger Hill, my daily forty-five degree uphill exercise. Coming down Harshbarger Hill was a thrill but going up was a challenge. The two of us could never manage either up or down, so that eliminated the last third.

The middle third of the route—from Bernie's house on Boggs Street to the south side of Main Street and on to Thatcherville Hill—had possibilities. Thatcherville Hill was the third-steepest incline in DeGraff but, I figured, was manageable. The middle of the paper route was perfect for Bernie.

When I explained my idea to him, he was a little miffed he'd not be experiencing the entire route but soon came around to liking the plan. He made me promise we'd use his wheelchair and not the wooden cart his dad had built for him several years before. When he was younger, Bernie's mom and dad pulled him up and down their street in the cart, but he was convinced he had outgrown it. I also think the cart embarrassed him, so I wasn't about to argue with him. We chose the next Saturday for our big adventure. Bernie got his mom's approval, and I ran it by my parents as well. Surprisingly, his mom agreed to let him go and even seemed pleased about our excursion.

I don't know if Bernie's mom was overly protective or not, but she was definitely protective. She had a right to be. Even as a kid, I understood why she feared for his safety. Because of her cautious nature, however, most of Bernie's grand plans for us never saw a glimmer of sunshine.

Creeks and ponds were her biggest fear, so fishing was

not an option no matter how hard Bernie begged. I didn't argue with Bernie's mother on his behalf, not even when he pleaded for me to do so. The image of a submerged Bernie strapped in his wheelchair made me a contented landlubber with a dry-docked Bernie.

As a result, Bernie's endlessly daydreamed adventures remained mostly unrealized musings, living alone with him within his narrow, small side yard. But on a couple of rare occasions, I was allowed to help Bernie escape from his world into a new one. Thatcherville Hill was definitely a new world.

I only had a few days to figure out our method of travel. At first, I thought I might be able to rig up some type of apparatus to hook Bernie to my bike and pull him, but I quickly rejected that as being too cumbersome. Besides, I wasn't sure how to go about it. I knew that Israel Gross, DeGraff's last blacksmith, had a harness we could use, but I didn't like the picture of me pulling a harnessed Bernie. I didn't want to look as though I were using Bernie to plow the sidewalks of DeGraff.

I finally decided simple was best. I'd leave my bike at Bernie's and push him house to house. I could then take him back to his house and finish the rest of the collections myself. The plan was workable, and I was admittedly pleased with myself for devising it.

I started my collections early that morning and arrived at Bernie's house about 9:00. He was sitting in the side yard with two paper bags and a thermos on his lap.

"What's that stuff?" I asked, clicking down the kickstand and parking my bicycle by his chair.

"Peanut butter sandwiches and lemonade," he replied proudly. "Mom thought we might need provisions."

No way would that work. I was going to have my hands full on this trip anyway without having to stop every few feet to pick up the sandwiches and thermos bouncing off his lap.

"Bernie, we won't need that. Snacks from customers while collecting come with the territory."

I stuffed the sandwich bags and thermos behind the shrubs in front of their house and the adventure began.

Our first stop was across the street at the Carters. I pushed Bernie up the front sidewalk and knocked on the door. Mrs. Carter was expecting me and had her thirty cents ready. When she saw Bernie, she smiled and said good morning, figuring I had merely wheeled him from across the street for a different view. She had no way of knowing her home was just the first leg of our expedition.

Next was Miss Lizzie Moore. I'd been worried about this stop. Bernie and I seldom talked about his condition, but I'm certain he didn't think of himself as being crippled.

Miss Lizzie came to the screen door and gave us both a quizzical look before addressing me. "Well, you have the boy from next door with you today." Even though she had lived by Bernie forever, she was meeting him for the first time.

"Yes, Miss Lizzie, this is Bernie Jones." She then did a remarkable thing, at least remarkable for her. She squeezed herself sideways out the barely-opened door and stood on the front porch beside us. Miss Lizzie looked different in the sunlight and out of the shadows of her door. She had porcelain skin and was dainty as a lawn statue.

"Very nice to meet you, Mr. Jones," she said with a slight curtsy, "I'm Lizzie." She reached out and caressed his forearm while handing me six nickels. "You gentlemen enjoy the rest of the day."

"Thanks, Miss Lizzie," I said. But she'd already disappeared back inside the house.

As I pushed him across the street to the next customer,

my friend Denny Allison's house, Bernie was smiling. "Miss Lizzie was nice."

"Yes, she was, Bernie. You bring out the best in people."

Some of my customers, including Denny's parents, left their money in a *Bellefontaine Examiner* envelope hung from the doorknob, making the collection stops routine. Seems funny by today's standards to think honesty and trust of that nature ever existed, but they did in DeGraff. I never once, in all my years of delivering newspapers, had money stolen.

After we left Bernie's world on Boggs Street and turned onto South Main, we were a couple of hundred yards from downtown DeGraff. Bernie asked me to stop pushing him, as he stared ahead at the two- and three-story brick and limestone buildings of DeGraff's business district. It was as if this was the first time he'd seen them. Turns out, in a way, it was.

"I've never seen DeGraff like this," he said. "We drive through town in the car, but this is different. I like it."

Bernie's speech pattern was oftentimes agonizingly slow, and he struggled to finish long sentences. I tried to be patient and let him work through the words at his own pace without finishing his sentences for him, even if I thought I knew what he was going to say. Most of the time I was able to keep quiet until he finished.

"Yeah, it is a nice sight from here," I said, standing behind him, my hands caressing the back of his wheelchair. We shared the view for another minute, and then I suggested moving on because we had a long way to go.

A couple of my customers on South Main made a big fuss over Bernie. Bill Shoemaker, Mayor of DeGraff for two decades before he retired, was a great storyteller and joker. Years as a politician do that to you. He told Bernie that when he was younger, he'd watched Bernie's house being built by Bill Baseore and other carpenters from the DeGraff Lumber Company. He said it was the finest house on Boggs Street. After a perfectly timed pause, he said it was about the only house on Boggs Street at the time, and we laughed, especially Bernie. As we were leaving, Mr. Shoemaker told Bernie that his dad was a fine and honest man, and I thought that was a great thing for Bernie to hear. Bernie was pleased and thanked him with a wobbly nod of his head.

Next were the Hostetlers who lived across the street from the Shoemakers. Mrs. Hostetler was usually waiting each Saturday for me with a plate of warm, freshly baked chocolate chip cookies and a small carton of cold milk. Her front porch was a nice place to take another break. The porch had several steps, too many for me to maneuver Bernie up, so Mrs. Hostetler and I carried down a couple of chairs and sat on either side of him. We lounged in the shade of a large sugar maple and ate the cookies and drank our glasses of milk. Like corporate executives, paperboys also have their perks.

As Mrs. Hostetler small-talked about the beautiful day, her vegetable garden, and flower patches, she included Bernie in the conversation with questions like, "Bernie, do your parents have a garden?" and "What's your favorite kind of flower, Bernie?" I liked the way she involved him. Bernie's answers, however, were short and unusually strained, and he did little to extend the conversation. I think he was nervous around pretty ladies, and Mrs. Hostetler was certainly attractive. By the time we left her house, I think Bernie liked her almost as much as he did Sparkle Plenty.

After a couple more customers, we pushed away from South Main. It was time to tackle Thatcherville Hill. This was not going to be easy, and I had mentally prepared

Bernie and myself for the challenge. I figured at some point, probably about three-quarters of the way up, I'd need to pull Bernie's wheelchair instead of pushing it. He didn't seem to mind when I explained the procedure to him, but I also doubt he had ever been in the position of looking down a steep incline while being pulled up. Disaster remained a distinct possibility. If I slipped or lost my grip on the handles of his chair, he'd have the soapbox derby ride of his life without the steering wheel or brakes of a soapbox racer. I had to be super careful.

I had watched *Kiss of Death*, a 1940s gangster film noir, on television a few weeks before, and its wheelchair scene still haunted me. Richard Widmark, playing the worst villain I'd ever seen, maniacally pushed an old lady in her wheelchair down a flight of stairs. I did not want to be remembered forever as the Rickie Widmark of DeGraff.

I had seven customers on the left going up Thatcherville, beginning with the Keenens and ending with Mr. and Mrs. Frantz, first-generation immigrants from Germany who owned a small vegetable market near the center of town. Eight customers were on the other side going down, starting with Ethel Mooring at the top all the way to Harry Nogle at the bottom. Usually, I'd ride my bike fast and recklessly down the rapid descent. Today, however, I needed to be slow and *wreckless*.

When Mrs. Keenen saw me hauling Bernie, she had a conniption fit. A very protective and cautious lady with two kids of her own, she reacted as mothers are prone to do, seeing only the dangers of our adventure and none of the benefits.

"Rickie, are you planning to roll him up Thatcherville?" she questioned, pointing upward toward the hill.

"Yes, ma'am, I am, but I have a plan." Crap, I sounded like a kid, and I could tell by the look on her face she didn't think I had any plan at all.

"Does your mother know what you're doing?" Her matronly arms were now folded and locked tight.

"Yes, ma'am, she knows all about it. So does my dad." Even though Mrs. Keenen liked my parents, my self-confidence was draining fast. Bernie wasn't any help as he sat there, voiceless, counting pebbles in their driveway. The first time I need his support and he becomes a pebble counter.

"If I called your mother right now, would she tell me she approves of this?"

Holy cow, Mrs. Keenen sounded like she did basic training under General George S. Patton!

"Yes, ma'am, she'd tell you it's okay with her."

Mrs. Keenen then unlocked her arms and in a surprisingly gentle voice said, "Then you be careful, very careful."

"Yes, ma'am, I will," I promised as I began wheeling Bernie toward the next house as carefully as if he were a crate of DeGraff Hatchery eggs.

The next four houses were uneventful. Two had envelopes hanging on the doorknobs with my money inside, while Lula Taylor didn't even notice Bernie and old Mr. Painter just waved toward him. I'm not certain Mr. Painter even knew what he was waving at because he was ancient with really thick glasses and could barely find his paper in the front bushes on those rare occasions when I'd miss his porch.

After the Painter house, I pivoted Bernie's wheelchair to pull him the rest of the way up Thatcherville Hill. When I turned him and he faced the downhill slope for the first time, I asked if he was okay. He didn't answer. I leaned forward to take a look at him. His eyes were as big as golf balls. He obviously now had some doubts about our plan.

But we were there and had nowhere to go but up. Neither of us said a word as we crept slowly up the hill step by step, roll by roll. I'll bet he never blinked until we reached Rita Thornton's house at the top.

In all the time I'd known Bernie, I'd never looked closely at his wheelchair until I began to tug it up the hill. The chair was solid and heavy with lots of chrome-plated metal, two large steel-rimmed back tires, and smaller all-rubber wheels in front that swiveled for turning. Behind his back was a large, thickly-folded towel, and he sat on a flat cushion extending side to side atop the stretched leather seat.

I suddenly realized the wheelchair was an integral part of Bernie's life and not merely an accessory to it. I felt bad I hadn't given his chair the proper respect before our adventure. Now, when I see someone in a wheelchair, I consider the chair to be an extension of the person in it. I don't know if that's a good or bad thing, but I do it nonetheless.

The Thornton house was my final collection on the upside of Thatcherville Hill. Rita Thornton was the sexiest girl in my class, all the way from first grade through high school, and I felt blessed to have her on my route. Her full name was Rita Ann Thornton and, because of her initials, she was nicknamed Rat. But she was definitely no rodent and was always Rita to me. She was extremely popular, a cheerleader, and on the homecoming court all four years of high school. Plus, she was a really nice girl.

When I was lucky, she'd be the one to pay me on Saturdays. As she talked nonstop about band or chorus—she played trumpet and sang soprano—I'd listen intently and fantasize. I think I was able to speed down Thatcherville Hill so quickly because, after a few minutes with Rita, my male hormone afterburners kicked in.

On this day, I was her hero for bringing Bernie with me. "Oh my gosh, Rick, this is so cool. I can't believe you brought him all the way up. You really are a great guy."

Yeah, Rita, I thought to myself, if I'm such a great guy, why are you dating Butch Helmandollar and not me? Explain that one. But when she brought out a box of gingersnap cookies, all was quickly forgiven.

Rita paid special attention to Bernie, and I admired her even more. For several months after our visit, Bernie asked about Rita, and I'd tell him she had asked about him as well. A few times, she actually had. Guys like Bernie and me appreciated being asked about by girls like Rita. Male insecurities run deep at any age.

As we left Rita and crossed the street to begin our collection descent, something unusual was happening below. I saw people standing on the sidewalks on both sides of the road down the hill. Mrs. Keenen had apparently called her neighbors and asked them to be on the lookout for us and to make sure we were okay.

As we came down the hill, some of my customers stationed themselves at the front and back of Bernie's wheelchair to help me with him. They all greeted him by name. Everyone wanted to talk with Bernie, so it took a while to reach Harry Nogle's house, the last customer on Thatcherville Hill. We hung around thanking everyone before saying our good-byes.

I pushed Bernie away as the hill flattened out into smooth road once again. We turned to look back. My customers were still outside laughing and talking with one another. "That's nice to see," I said aloud before turning Bernie around for the ride back to his house.

Bernie talked most of the way back, reliving our adventure as he always loved to do. I think Bernie met more people that day than he had in his entire life. It had been an eventful excursion, but I could tell he was tired.

Just before we reached his house, straight out of the blue Bernie blurted out, "She called you Rick."

"What? What are you talking about?"

"Up at her house, Rita called you Rick."

"Yeah, so what? So what if she called me Rick?"

Bernie's reply was so earnest, I was caught completely off guard. "Do you want me to call you Rick?"

Bernie always surprised me. The way he processed things and thought about stuff was way different than anyone I knew and certainly not the way I did. After several years of friendship, he was now concerned about what to call me. He was really something.

"No, Bernie," I assured him, "you can still call me Rickie. In fact, I'd prefer it." At that time in my life, I was Rick more often than I was Rickie and, being the typical kid who wanted to grow up quickly, I kind of liked the more adult-sounding Rick. But with Bernie, I preferred being called Rickie.

"Good," he said, grinning his silly grin, "because Rick, my boy, doesn't sound so hot."

"No, Bernie, it doesn't."

"But Rickie, my boy, does." He rolled his eyes, pleased with himself. "Rickie, my boy, does."

I grabbed the sandwiches Mrs. Jones had made for us from behind the bushes, emptied the thermos, and sat it on the porch. It was after 1:00 p.m., and I was really running late and still had the last third of my route to collect as well as the afternoon papers to deliver. I put my hand on Bernie's shoulder. "Great day, buddy, great day we had."

Bernie wobbled his head in agreement and repeated what I'd said. "Great day, buddy, great day we had."

I pedaled away, scattering gravel right and left, and dropped the peanut butter sandwiches in a big trash bin by the box factory's main entrance.

40

The next day after lunch, Jeff and I were tossing a baseball back and forth in the front yard. Mr. Bethel, our across-the-street neighbor and school superintendent, an awkward combination for my family, walked to the edge of his driveway and called my name.

"Rick, I would like to talk to you for a couple of minutes."

"Sure, Mr. Bethel," I hollered while throwing the ball back to Jeff. Unsure of what he wanted, I held onto my glove like a security blanket just in case I was in some kind of trouble. As I jogged across the street toward Mr. Bethel, I could see he was smiling, so I figured I must not have done anything too bad.

"How are you doing today, Mr. Bethel?" I asked adult-like. "How was church?"

"I am very well, thank you, and our minister had a wonderful message. Let's have a seat around back. I want to talk to you."

We walked through the garage to the back patio where four redwood chairs were placed around a picnic table on which were two ice-filled glasses and a sweating pitcher of sun tea. I removed my baseball glove and slid it under my chair.

Mr. Bethel filled the glasses, and we sat for a moment without speaking. I gulped at my tea while he sipped his properly.

He broke the silence. "At church this morning, Mrs. Bethel and I heard about what you did for the Jones boy yesterday."

As I've mentioned, there were no secrets in DeGraff, and nothing went unnoticed. Husbands dare not sneak around

Rick D. Niece, Ph.D.

on their wives, and wives dare not wink at the deliverymen.

"It really wasn't anything, Mr. Bethel. I just took Bernie around with me on part of my paper route. Really, it wasn't anything."

"Yes, Rick, it was. It truly was. Your gesture was a very special one."

Adults always seem to read more than there is into a kid thing, sometimes for the better and sometimes for the worse. This was one of those over-read readings.

"Really, Mr. Bethel, it was nothing great. Bernie wanted to see part of my newspaper route, so I took him with me."

Mr. Bethel smiled the kind of smile adults do when they think they know more than you know but don't want to embarrass you.

"Rick, I want you to listen carefully to what I am about to say. No interruptions until I am finished. Will you agree?" I nodded. "I am going to ask a favor from you." He paused to take another sip of tea. "In a few years you will have a big decision to make, and as you are making it, I hope you will remember this request." He looked straight into my eyes as he spoke. "I want you to be a teacher. You have a kind heart, you care about people, and you do well in school. Those are the traits of an effective teacher, and I think you would be a fine one."

I really hadn't given much thought to what I wanted to be. Several years before, I had told my Uncle Robert I wanted to be a professional whistler. I hadn't improved my technique since then, however, so whistling for a living was probably out. Being a teacher hadn't entered my mind. Besides, I could never be as good a teacher as my dad, and comparisons to him would probably hound me from school to school my whole teacher life.

But I really did feel complimented by Mr. Bethel's words and his confidence in me. Except he was mostly wrong.

42

I wasn't very kindhearted, and I only cared about certain people. But I was a good student, so he had a third of me right.

"Thank you, Mr. Bethel. I promise I'll consider it." And I think I really meant it, although I could not look him as straight in the eye as he had me.

He refilled my glass. I leaned back in the chair and sipped like a proper gentleman.

CHAPTER SIX

RULES AND ETIQUETTE OF CROQUET

Not all of my encounters with Mr. Bethel were pleasant ones. From the very beginning, my father was apprehensive about the Bethels living not only in our neighborhood but directly across the street from us. When Jack and Velma Boone moved out and Emery and Betty Bethel moved in, Dad became a nervous wreck, and for good reason. Mr. Bethel was the superintendent where Dad taught music and where his boys attended school. The day the moving van arrived and the Bethels began to unpack was the day I heard my dad use a variation of the word "awkward" three times in the same sentence.

"No doubt about it. The awkwardness of this awkwardly situation is going to be unbelievably awkward!"

From his worrisome look and this doomsday uttering, I gathered having the DeGraff school superintendent across the street was going to put a big dent in our previously uninhibited lives. I wasn't too concerned about me. No, I was worried about Jeff and Kurt. You never knew what they might do or say to embarrass the family and cause Dad to lose his job. At least, those were my thoughts on the dilemma. I later learned that Dad had not singled out any of us, realizing that his sons or his wife or even he was capable of bringing down the family. The school executive head was living across the street from us, and we were preparing for the worst. This could be awkward.

Without a doubt, the Bethels added class to our neighborhood. It isn't as if we weren't a refined group already, but after watching them, we realized we were only small-town refined. Mr. Bethel remains one of few intellectuals who influenced my life, seeing potential in me that eluded other people's observations. Even with my promising potential, however, life around Mr. Bethel was not always smooth.

The competitive nature of my family is well documented. None of us gives an inch, and Mom is as fiercely competitive as any among us but simply won't admit it. A pleasant Sunday afternoon game of croquet, two weeks after our new neighbors moved in, gave Mr. Bethel his first indication of the Niece clan clamor.

Green is my favorite color, and I'd always use the green mallet and the green-striped ball for our croquet matches. For some reason on that Sunday, Jeff laid claim to them first. The blue ball and mallet were his usual choice, except when he was being contrary. This was one of his contrary days. Dad was in no mood for our sibling squabbles, so Jeff was allowed to keep the green, and I was stuck with blue and developed an even bluer attitude.

I don't remember exactly how it started, but suddenly and with the intensity of a grease fire on a stove, the five of us were at one another, including Kurt, who was shorter than his mallet and just learning the game. One of us usually remained in control to serve as mediator, but not this time. We were all yelling at once with no one listening. Not a word was understandable anyway.

I was still blabbing on, having not realized the rest of

my family was in mute-button silence. I then noticed Mr. Bethel had slipped into our group. He shook his head in wonderment, handed my dad something, and left without a word. The mute button released, we noisily gathered around Dad to see what Mr. Bethel had delivered. In Dad's shaking hand was a small booklet entitled *The Rules and Etiquette of Croquet.* We stared at it awkwardly.

Later that evening, we had a study session to master the booklet, followed by a thorough review and capped off with a quiz. Kurt was the only family member to pass.

The Bethel house was a relatively modest one before they moved in, with nothing distinctive to make it stand out from the rest of the Mill Street homes. But once they occupied it, the transformation was impressive. They added fresh paint, fancy shutters, new slate shingles, a resurfaced asphalt driveway, and artistic landscaping. The renovations occurred during the summer, and the process was amazing to watch. Once they finished, everything looked meticulous except for an out-of-control, fenced in half-acre behind their perfectly manicured backyard. The area was fondly known as the apple orchard, but the orchard hadn't seen a decent apple since Johnny Appleseed was a seedling—no upkeep, no produce.

Soon after the Bethels arrived, my mother proudly informed them that I was required to save four dollars a week from the paper route toward my college education. It was true. Every week, I dutifully saved four dollars toward my higher education. At the time, of course, I groused, grumbled, and pleaded for an exemption, but none was ever granted. As I look back, my parental-imposed savings plan was the best lesson in financial discipline I ever received.

Rick D. Niece, Ph.D.

One day, when I was in the front yard trying to teach Lady to count like Fern Burdette's Duke, Mr. Bethel walked over and asked if I wanted to earn some extra money. When the superintendent speaks, you pay attention. I asked what he had in mind. He said he had heard about my college savings plan and guessed I could use a little extra spending money for myself. You had to hand it to him, the man was perceptive.

"Tell you what," he proposed, "I will give you ten dollars to whip the apple orchard into shape and then five dollars every other week to keep it mowed and trimmed." A big smile gave away my euphoria.

I kept my end of the agreement, and the apple orchard soon looked as presentable as the rest of the Bethel property. The first whacks at it took most of a prime summer weekend, but from then on the maintenance was like a biweekly trim in the barbershop.

One lazy afternoon before I was about to start mowing the orchard, Mrs. Bethel invited me into their house for a glass of iced tea. Carrying our glasses on a silver tray, she led me into the den where Mr. Bethel was already seated. There I saw the reason I'd been invited in. Before me in all of its glory was the grandest high fidelity record playing system I'd ever seen. Mr. Bethel was understandably proud, and "His Master's Voice" had a most appreciative master.

"Are you familiar with Tchaikovsky's *1812 Overture*?" he asked.

"I sure am," I replied, relieved he'd asked me about a classical piece I liked and not some obscure aria from an opera. I never wanted to bluff my way through anything with Mr. Bethel.

"Have you heard the overture the way Tchaikovsky wrote it to be played, with actual cannon shots instead of using timpani?"

48

"No, sir," I said, now in awe. "Actual cannon shots?"

"Yes, the *1812 Overture* was written to commemorate Napoleon's failed attempt to overthrow the Russian Empire. Tchaikovsky used the salvos of cannon shots to represent Russia's successful resistance."

I already knew the story behind the overture, but Mr. Bethel sounded so professorial I felt like I was hearing it for the first time. He lifted the diamond-needled arm, placed it gently on the record, and Mr. Tchaikovsky's wondrous work filled the room. In our house, the only source for classical music was a small, gray vinyl-covered Silvertone Tru-Phonic Phonograph that scratched out nearly recognizable monophonic sounds from Dad's collection of classical recordings. But the Silvertone's tiny speakers were no match for Mr. Bethel's golden-toned ones. I have never been more transfixed. For seventeen glorious minutes, I was in a concert hall with Peter Ilyich Tchaikovsky and the London Philharmonic.

About three quarters through the overture, I knew the cannon blasts were mere measures away. The first cannon rattled the ice cubes in my tea, and they kept rattling at every blast. As the long final crescendo began and the victory bells chimed in followed by the second series of cannon shots, I could feel the vibrations in the glass of iced tea I held in my hand. The cannons echoed through me. And then silence. After a respectful pause, Mr. Bethel asked what I thought. He could tell by my loss-for-words expression that I was unable to explain the beauty of what I had just experienced.

"I understand," he said, nodding. "The music leaves me speechless as well. You can replay it in your head, again and again, as you mow the orchard."

And I did replay it—each note, each measure, each cannon shot. Fantasizing about a career as the first chair whistler for the London Philharmonic, I mowed the last swatch just as I whistled my full crescendo big finish. Uncle Robert would have been proud.

CHAPTER SEVEN

AMONG THE ENTREPRENEURS

All small towns have their own gathering places for social gossip and friendly chatter. One of DeGraff's popular spots was Taylor's Restaurant near the center of downtown and across the street from the DeGraff Public Library. Run by Wig and Becky Taylor, the restaurant did a brisk business with hometown regulars throughout the day. Becky was a superb cook, especially when it came to her hamburgers, and Wig was an exemplary host/waiter/cashier/busboy/host. The two of them ran the whole show with occasional assistance from their daughter, Cat.

Wintry Saturdays were my favorite times to stop at Taylor's Restaurant. Halfway through collecting for the weekly paper, I'd hurry in to warm up with a steaming cup of Becky's hot chocolate. (Thankfully, packets of instant hot chocolate had not yet reached rural Ohio.)

Becky made her hot chocolate from scratch, magically mixing milk, cream, sugar, butter, and thick bars of semisweet chocolate in an iron pan on the stove and coaxing the dark brown ambrosia to a perfect simmer. She'd then carefully ladle her elixir into marshmallow-laded, wide-brim mugs for Wig to serve awaiting customers. These breaks from the cold weather were special times.

One extremely frigid, double-digit below zero Saturday

morning, I clumped into Taylor's numbed and icicled. I had been dreaming of Becky's hot chocolate since my first steps outside, and that vision kept me from freezing stiff. Wig greeted me at the counter with grim reaper news.

"No hot chocolate today, Rickie. Becky's down with the flu and Cat's cooking, but she won't consider attempting her mother's hot chocolate. How about a cup of my java?"

I hadn't been that disappointed since the Christmas I'd expected a puppy and Mom and Dad brought home my baby brother Jeff instead. Coffee instead of hot chocolate? How about liver instead of lasagna? Brussels sprouts instead of brownies? Ma Kettle instead of Annette Funicello? I'd only had one drink of coffee in my life, and that singular sip was more than enough to last a lifetime. I could not imagine consuming an entire cup of the stuff. Coffee instead of hot chocolate? No way!

But my brain was frozen. "Sure," I answered, cold and desperate. "Sure, pour me a cup."

I don't know if it was the disappointment of not having Becky's hot chocolate or if it was simply that Wig Taylor didn't know beans about making a decent cup of java. I don't know what it was. But that swallow forever ruined coffee for me. I haven't tasted a drop since. I don't even like Kahlúa.

DeGraff's prominent leaders were frequent visitors to Taylor's and many business deals—the consequential as well as the insignificant—were conceived and born there. I enjoyed sipping my hot chocolate at the counter while watching the impressive paper shuffling going on in one of the corner booths. Fantasizing about the economic windfalls my small town would soon reap from these big transactions, I was honored to be a mere paperboy seated among this cavalcade of entrepreneurs.

A few years before my newspaper delivering days,

I'd had my first experience with a real entrepreneur, my Granddad Niece. He and my grandmother owned The Urban Store, a small clothing store in a town several miles from DeGraff.

Often on Saturdays, when I was five, my dad and I would travel to their rustic boutique. Through the eyes of a young boy, the store seemed like a gigantic, big city Macy's. In reality, it was merely a small, mom-and-pop all-purpose clothing store.

My dad assisted with taking the inventory on Saturdays, and I'd be left to walk in wonderment through the mystical maze of aisles and narrow passageways magically created by the racks of clothing. The store was a garmented field sown with row after row of multicolored fabrics and designs all ripe and ready for the shoppers to harvest.

Each Saturday, I found myself drawn to a well-lit corner at the back of the store where there was a big display of shoes—all styles, shapes, sizes, and shades. I noticed that the display was different from week to week. That is, except for one pair. This same pair of dark brown men's shoes sat in the exact same spot week after week.

After several months, I finally decided to examine them. I had no idea what I was looking for when I cautiously picked up one of the shoes. Its dusty outline remained on the display shelf, and I realized, in my slow-to-comprehend little boy reasoning, that these shoes had not been moved for a long time. Holding the brown shoe in both hands, I ran to the front of the store to find my grandfather and tell him about my amazing discovery.

I found him in his office sifting through stacks of bills and receipts, and I rushed up to him excitedly. I asked him why the pair of shoes had remained on the shelf for so long. He smiled and gently took the shoe from me. He motioned for me to sit beside him in his leather desk chair.

53

I'd always been fascinated by his office. A picture of a man in a cowboy hat hung on the wall above his massive rolltop desk. I'd asked him once who the man was, and he told me it was his idol, Will Rogers. I asked if Will Rogers could be my idol, too, and he generously said we could share him.

As we sat there in his chair, he shared his secret about the shoe. He turned it over slowly in his hands a few times before explaining he'd never cared much for this pair of shoes. A regional salesman from the Florsheim company, however, had talked him into buying them, convincing him the shoes were the newest rage in men's footwear. (The salesman obviously did not know fashion trends in rural Ohio.) Against his better entrepreneurial instincts, my grandfather bought the pair.

He lovingly squeezed my shoulder and shared an insight I've never forgotten. He said he'd left the shoes on display to remind him never again to try to sell something he didn't believe in himself. Those were powerful words for a little boy to understand, but over time I've grasped the meaning of his lesson.

My grandfather and I walked back to the display and put the shoe carefully within the dusty pattern on the shelf. The shoes remained unsold until his death and the store's eventual closing. Will Rogers never met a man he didn't like. I know he'd have especially liked my grandfather, the first real entrepreneur in my life.

So I felt at ease on Saturdays, sipping Becky Taylor's rich hot chocolate while sharing a work break with DeGraff's entrepreneurs. Although we didn't exactly rub shoulders, we did drink from the same mugs.

Gil Mooring, president and owner of the People's Building & Loan, was a no-nonsense businessman and a restaurant regular, and his mother was a customer on my paper route. Through the two of them, I was about to learn another unforgettable lesson.

DeGraff is a rural area surrounded by dozens of small, family-owned farms. Making a living from the land is a constant struggle for the hard-working families held hostage by Ohio's fickle weather. Back then, farmers often needed second and third mortgages to stay afloat. Gil Mooring was their ready savior and quickly became the major lender in town, gaining the trust of the farming community.

His mother, Ethel Mooring, lived at the top of the west side of Thatcherville Hill. Her home was the newest one in the neighborhood, all brick with white shuttered windows. Gil had it built for her after his father's death. Although a delightful and engaging lady, she had none of her son's financial sense. Collecting from her was always a challenge, as she'd insist on either under- or overpaying me. She remembered when the paper was a dime for the week or she'd think it was fifty cents, with never much common ground in between. One Saturday, Mr. Mooring was visiting his mother as I was attempting to collect, and he quickly got the picture. After Mrs. Mooring and I settled on thirty cents for the fourth time, he walked me to my bicycle.

He stood there with his hands in his pockets, posing as though he was about to address a business colleague, and then laid out a plan. "Tell you what. Why don't you just stop by my office each week, and I will pay you for

Mother's paper. That should save you the frustration and her the time. Agreed?"

I liked his idea immediately and thought it would work. But it didn't. An even bigger problem soon developed. He was seldom available when I stopped by the People's Building & Loan to collect. He was either out of his office or in with a client. I guess I was no longer his business colleague because when I told the secretary I was his "newspaper proprietor" and needed to see him on personal business, she didn't even suggest an appointment. Instead, she smiled and handed me a lollipop.

After several weeks, the bill reached what was for me enormous proportions. The Moorings now owed me $2.10! A significant part of my weekly profit was somewhere in Gil Mooring's pocket.

One afternoon when I was delivering the newspapers, I saw him leaving Taylor's Restaurant, and did a quick U-turn and pedaled up to him. "Mr. Mooring, I'd like to collect for the paper," I said innocently. I was about to learn a lesson.

Gil Mooring was incensed and took a moment to compose himself. He inhaled a deep breath and began to lecture me.

"Listen to me, young man, and listen very carefully. A gentleman never asks another gentleman for money on the street. Business transactions are not conducted in that manner. A gentleman always requests money in private. Financial dealings are personal matters."

He stopped and searched my face for a reaction.

"Do you understand?"

I remember thinking that Will Rogers must never have met Gil Mooring.

"Yes, Mr. Mooring, I understand, and I'm sorry I asked you in public for the money you owe me. I won't do it again, sir." My parents had taught me to respect my elders.

"Good, then we have an understanding," he said, turning toward the People's Building & Loan. "Now, I have an appointment, and a businessman is never late for an appointment." With that, he was gone.

I learned two important lessons that day. First, never publicly ask a gentleman for money. Second, never be late for an appointment. Despite this valuable education, I was still out $2.10. I think that's when I began to learn my own lesson: Get 'em while you got 'em or they're gonna be gone.

The next week I made an official appointment through Mr. Mooring's secretary. She tried to put me off, but I was persistent and twice refused her offer of a cherry lollipop. After he paid me the new total of $2.40, we agreed to another plan. He'd leave the money for his mother's paper with his secretary, and I'd collect from her. That plan worked, and I looked forward each week to guessing what flavor lollipop I'd be offered.

A couple of months later, as I was nursing a hot chocolate in the back corner booth and carefully reviewing my ledger of customer collections, Gil Mooring strolled into Taylor's Restaurant, sat at the counter, and ordered a cup of coffee. When I paid Wig for my hot chocolate, I included a dime for Gil Mooring's coffee. As I opened the door to leave, I gave him a tip of my baseball cap, and he smiled. I think he was impressed. I know Will would have been.

CHAPTER EIGHT

TRICK OR TREAT WITH *THE DAILY PLANET*

I felt lucky to be a paperboy. The pay was steady at ten cents a week per customer (with seventy-two customers that was a cool $7.20). Four dollars of my weekly profit was put toward college, but the remaining $3.20 went a long way in DeGraff's modest cost of living economy. I didn't exactly live high on the hog—with twenty-five-cent movie tickets, ten-cent comic books, and nickel RC Colas and candy bars being among my extravagances—but I was almost up to a pig's rib cage.

As a paperboy, I also enjoyed professional perks. For one thing, my customers kept me well fed with cookies, pies, cakes, brownies, and apple dumplings. My favorite, though, was Miss Lizzie Moore's pumpkin bread. She baked brick-sized loaves to golden brown perfection and wrapped each one carefully in aluminum foil. On holidays only Miss Lizzie seemed to celebrate—like Groundhog Day, Arbor Day, and Armistice Day ending World War I—through her barely opened screen door, she would offer me a foiled loaf along with my weekly payment. Miss Lizzie celebrated holidays the rest of us forgot while never seeming to remember the notable ones.

Miss Lizzie was a curiosity of legendary status in

DeGraff. Few citizens had ever seen her in public. My only not-through-the-screen-door glimpse of her had been that Saturday Bernie and I collected for the paper when she stepped beyond the door of her small world and into the outside universe of ours. The reclusive Miss Lizzie was DeGraff's Emily Dickinson.

According to Sam Hamsher, DeGraff's unofficial resident historian who knew a little bit of something about everyone in town, Miss Lizzie once worked in a mail sorting car for the New York Central Railroad. The train used to pass daily on the tracks by Bernie's house and by the box factory long before either was constructed. Miss Lizzie sorted mail with a man named Dewey Daniel Stanton, nicknamed Dewstan by his paternal grandfather.

As sometimes happens when two people work within close proximity, they became friendly, courted, and fell in love. One late October afternoon, the train made its usual stop for coal and water at the DeGraff Depot (a structure razed three decades later to make way for the box factory). In a quiet corner of the Depot, Dewstan asked Miss Lizzie to marry him. She accepted, and they planned a June wedding for the following summer in 1917.

Fate, however, intervened. The United States entered World War I on April 6, 1917. They postponed their wedding because Dewstan enlisted in the Army and was shipped overseas. The following year, Dewey Daniel Stanton was killed in France as he and his doughboy comrades defended the Marne River Line at Chateau-Thierry.

Miss Lizzie quit her railroad mailroom job and built a small house near the Depot where Dewstan had proposed. And there she lived to old age, receiving *The Bellefontaine Examiner* six days a week, seldom venturing beyond her front door.

I liked Miss Lizzie and respected her solitude. In time, she began to like me as well. After we'd have a conversation, always shared through her screen door, I'd be rewarded the following day with a loaf of pumpkin bread. I guess it became one of those special holidays only Miss Lizzie wanted to celebrate.

During my junior year in high school and the week before Halloween, Miss Lizzie made a startling request when I stopped to collect for the paper. Her request was a doozy. She asked if Bernie and I would help her give out treats to the trick-or-treaters. This fragile, cloistered whisper of a lady who barely opened her door to me wanted to celebrate Halloween by encouraging pint-sized goblins, pirates, and witches to knock on her door. I cannot imagine the look on my face when she asked me to assist.

I finally managed to stammer, "What are you going to give them, Miss Lizzie?"

She looked as stunned at my question as I had at her request. "Why, young man, it's Halloween. I think pumpkin bread is the perfect treat for Halloween, don't you?" Who was I to question the obvious?

I could not wait to tell Bernie. He lived for out-of-the-ordinary stuff like this. Celebrating Halloween with Miss Lizzie was certainly bound to make the top ten out-of-the-ordinary events on his fantasy list of potential adventures. After I told him about Miss Lizzie, Bernie caught me off guard with a question.

"But, Rickie, my boy, what are we going to be?"

I was at a loss for words, and so Bernie repeated himself with unmistakable clarity. "What are we going to wear? Who are we going to dress up like?"

Costumes! I hadn't even considered costumes. Before I could give his question any creative thought, he answered for both of us.

61

Rick D. Niece, Ph.D.

"I've got it! I'll be Superman, and you'll be Clark Kent."

Superman was Bernie's second favorite hero, next in line to Dick Tracy. He'd been a fan of the television program, *The Adventures of Superman*, for several years and was still disappointed at its cancellation. The program's simplistic plots revolved around Superman's heroics in Metropolis, the newspaper offices of *The Daily Planet*, and the inept but lovable reporters Clark Kent, Lois Lane, and Jimmy Olson. I think Bernie had a crush on Lois Lane, but I could never get him to admit it.

I tried my best to reason with him. "But, Bernie, Clark Kent and Superman are the same person. You and I do not look enough alike for you to be Superman and me Clark Kent. Besides, the two of them couldn't be in a room together because they were the same guy, Bernie. How are you and I going to pass out treats together in the same room as the same guy?"

He gave me an icy stare. I felt as though he'd caught me selling Kryptonite to gangsters. I'd learned over the years not to argue with him, as my reasoned logic seldom held a ghost of a chance against his illogical logic. After he'd made up his mind about something, there was no unmaking it. This was one of those no-unmaking situations.

"Okay, Bernie, you be Superman, and I'll be Clark Kent. But what about Miss Lizzie?"

I knew I had him.

He paused a Bernie pause, one of those rare instances when his eyes would unfocus and roam beyond me. After he gathered his thoughts, he began flapping his arms and legs. "She'll be Lois Lane! We'll stick a pencil behind her ear and give her a notebook."

And that was that. This Halloween was going to be trick-or-treat night with *The Daily Planet*.

62

As I delivered the paper each day leading up to Halloween, Miss Lizzie greeted me from behind the screen door and beckoned me toward her with an enticing invitation. "Try this batch of pumpkin bread, hot from the oven."

She'd hand me a slice, freshly buttered and snuggled on a napkin, and study me with her head cocked slightly, waiting for me to swallow. "Miss Lizzie, this is delicious. It may be the best one yet."

It may well have been. In all the years I sampled her pumpkin bread, I honestly never knew if one loaf was better than another. They were all superb month after month, year after year. The day before Halloween, after serving as official taste tester during the week before our grand giveaway, I asked the question that had been nagging at me.

"Miss Lizzie, how many loaves are you baking?" She winked. "Just enough, I'm certain, just enough." I had no idea how to quantify "just enough" and doubted she did either.

As I delivered Bernie's paper on the day of our big night, he was in full excitement overload and not the least bit interested in *Dick Tracy*. For that day Dick was on his own pursuing bad guys. "What time you coming back, Rickie, my boy?"

DeGraff's traditional time for kids and their parents to trick or treat was from 7:00 p.m. to 8:30 p.m. I figured I needed at least an hour before the costumed arrivals to push Bernie to Miss Lizzie's and help prepare for the onslaught of little beggars.

"I'll be back around six, Bernie. Is your Superman

costume ready?"

He cast a sideways, sheepish-eyed glance fairly close to my direction.

"Yeah, I guess."

Any lack of excitement, especially on a night like this, wasn't Bernie-like, and his subdued mood was way out of character.

"What do you mean, you guess?"

"You'll see, Rickie, you'll see."

When I returned an hour later to wheel him to Miss Lizzie's, I saw the source of his concern. My Clark Kent disguise was extremely minimal, consisting only of a pair of my dad's oversized, outdated horn-rimmed glasses with the lenses removed. Miss Lizzie's Lois Lane was extremely practical with a yellow, freshly sharpened number two pencil to stick behind her ear and a Hytone spiral notebook to tuck into her apron. And Bernie?

Well, Bernie as Superman was a combination of minimal, practical, and outright comically embarrassing. Superman Bernie, DeGraff's superhero for the evening, wore a cape consisting of his dad's red flannel long johns tied by the sleeves around his neck, the buttoned trapdoor and legs dangling over the back of his chair.

Unsuccessfully stifling my laughter, I tried my best to convince Bernie he looked superhero worthy. He didn't buy it and let me know how he felt about my disingenuousness with a sarcastic, "Yeah, right!"

He was right. Sitting there with his face as red as the underwear wrapped around his neck, Bernie looked pretty silly. In fact, all three of us would probably look silly. But on this Halloween night, my favorite Halloween of all time, it didn't matter.

I pushed Bernie to Miss Lizzie's and onto the front porch. The screen door and front door were propped open, allowing me to roll Bernie into Miss Lizzie's secret world.

The interior was neat and well kept. Everything looked comfortably in place except for the dining room table that had been moved close to the front door, lines of table leg tracks still visible on the carpet from being dragged across it. My eyes followed the tracks to a small bay window and four dimples in the carpet where the table's feet had obviously rested for a long time before their short journey.

On top of the linen-laced table was a perfectly triangular-shaped stack of foil-covered pumpkin loaves, mounded as carefully as the gold bars stored in Fort Knox and every bit as precious. I mentally tried to count them but kept losing track.

"Miss Lizzie, how many loaves did you bake?"

Again she answered simply, "Enough."

She smiled at the piled-high table, at Bernie, and then at me. As she did, I carefully examined, as I had never done before, the face framing her smile. I'd seen her face hundreds of times through the screen door and once in the sunlight on the porch, but I'd never looked closely at Miss Lizzie until now. Her delicately cast face reminded me of the one on a cameo brooch my father bought in Naples for my mother during World War II, warmly pink and finely detailed. I saw, even after all those years, why Dewey Daniel Stanton had fallen in love with her.

Bernie broke into my impolite inspection with an urgent insistence. "Rickie, my boy, give Miss Lizzie her costume!"

I handed Miss Lizzie the pencil and spiral notebook I'd brought with me. She was amused and cooperative while having no earthly idea who Lois Lane was. I doubt she'd ever heard of Superman and assumed, looking at Bernie, he was simply a man in a wheelchair who wore long underwear around his neck.

We still had half an hour before show time, so Miss

Lizzie cut a freshly baked pumpkin loaf into four fat slabs and thickly lathered each one with butter. A pitcher of milk shared a tarnished silver tray with three large mugs. I poured the milk for all of us and helped Bernie with his portions. Miss Lizzie nibbled at her bread politely while Bernie and I devoured ours like we had missed supper.

While chomping into my second slice, I noticed a small cherrywood table in the back corner of the living room. On it was a metal lamp with tasseled fringe around the rose-colored shade. Carefully placed beneath the lamp were several items, and I walked over to look more closely.

The table was actually an old-fashioned writing desk with a built-in inkwell and worn quill pen. I saw three military medals and a faded red, white, and blue ribbon hanging around a black and white photograph of a solemn-faced doughboy. A Bible was opened to Psalms, and a yellow Western Union telegram lay there between the pages now parchment-like from not being turned for many years. Beside the Bible in a yarn-wrapped collection were several letters, the top one with a French postmark and stamp. I tilted my head trying to read the address.

"I never opened the last of his letters." Miss Lizzie had been watching me. She paused before explaining what was none of my business. "As long as they remain unopened, I do not have to respond."

She folded her hands in her lap, and nothing more was said. I returned to my chair and the three of us sat in silence. As we waited for our visitors, I fed Bernie the rest of his pumpkin bread. The quiet was eventually interrupted by a tiny knock at the door that brought us back to Halloween. They were here.

The masquerade parade had begun and what a parade it was! We assembly-lined our giveaway process so efficiently that Henry Ford would have been proud. Except our "tin lizzies" were a different model than his and crafted by a single set of hands. Miss Lizzie guided the loaves onto Bernie's waiting lap, and I took them from there and placed them gently into the trick-or-treaters' sacks.

Word about the generous treats at Miss Lizzie's must have spread town-wide because I will swear it was as though every DeGraff household was eventually at her door. I'm pretty sure even childless adults were borrowing their neighbors' kids to lead them to our bounty. Kids as shills were a rarity in DeGraff, but on this night shilling was forgiven. I even saw two station wagons filled with kids from Quincy, the neighboring town.

No one noticed our costumes, or at least no one mentioned them, until the evening was almost over. As I was placing a shiny loaf into the bag of a little princess, she looked inside the house and saw Bernie.

"Daddy, look! It's Superman!" Her father peeked inside, smiled, and shook his head, looking equally amazed and bewildered. It didn't matter. That one moment of affirmation was all Bernie needed. I patted him on the shoulder and straightened his flowing cape over the wheelchair.

Astonishingly, the very last knock of the evening received the very last pumpkin loaf. Miss Lizzie's "enough," like my Grandma Ruth's pinch of salt and sprinkle of sugar, turned out to be exactly right.

We sat for several minutes, smugly proud and reminiscing about our busy evening and debating which children were the most creatively dressed. Bernie was unusually quiet. Knowing him as I did, I understood the reason. The end of something anxiously anticipated was always diffcult for him because it signaled the return to his daily routine of the ordinary.

As we were about to say our good nights, Miss Lizzie

went into the kitchen and returned with two neatly folded Fuson's IGA grocery bags. She handed me one and placed the other on Bernie's lap.

"I'll bet you thought I had forgotten you. Trick or treat!"

I opened my bag, and nested inside were four foiled loaves tied together by a ribbon and a bow.

Miss Lizzie leaned down and kissed Bernie on the cheek. "Bless you, Bernie, bless you." She opened the front door and held the screen door wide for me to wheel him through. As I did, she put her arm around my waist and pulled me close to her. I felt the rhythm of her heart through her ever-tightening grasp.

"Thank you for a wonderful week, my friend."

I turned to kiss her forehead, but before I could reach her, she had moved away and was already back inside.

"Good night, Miss Lizzie. Thanks for the pumpkin bread," was all I could manage before the front door closed.

Bernie and I didn't speak as I wheeled him toward his house. When we reached the porch, the light came on and Bernie's mother opened the door. She took the chair's handles and maneuvered him inside.

As I was walking away, Bernie called out, "Rickie, that little girl, she knew I was Superman!"

I turned toward him. "Yes she did, Bernie, yes she did. Your costume was perfect, buddy, the best of the evening. Good night."

The Halloween moon was not quite full, but the light was bright enough to extend the shadows to twice their size. I came to the railroad tracks and quickened my pace to cross them, but in mid-track I heard the blast of a train whistle. That was strange because no trains passed through DeGraff at that time of night. I froze and looked down the tracks in the direction of the sound. Just beyond the shadows' reach, I saw the pale figure of a man in uniform facing me. The whistle blew again, this time sounding even closer, and the penumbral silhouette drifted backward into the enfolding shadows.

I blinked twice to refocus my eyes, trying to recapture the image and disbelieve the unbelievable. I couldn't.

Clutching the grocery sack and my dad's lensless glasses, I jumped over the rest of the tracks and sprinted all the way home, looking back only once.

LETTERS

I enjoy rereading
     letters from
     Pliny the Younger,
     the Apostle Paul,
     Robert Browning and Elizabeth Barrett,
     Mark Twain,
     Martin Luther King,
     and my great-great-grandparents.

I am not embarrassed about
     being a benign interloper,
     curious and distant,
     officious yet respectful.
Letters
     become public readings
        of private lives
           as primary sources.
Letters
     sent to generations
     in their time,
     now for generations
     through time,
     correspond to me.

Letters of
     love
        hope
           passion
     peace
        fear
           remorse.

Letters,
>>>the bookmarks
>>>>>of times past
>>>>revived again by us
>>>>>who snoop.

Even letters
>>>>never opened
>>>>never read
leave a message
mystically strong and painful.

What letters
>>>>will this generation
>>>>>>leave as a legacy?

Who will carefully
>>>>yarn wrap and double bow
text messages?

CHAPTER NINE

THE GREAT HAMBURGER-EATING CONTEST

Taylor's Restaurant was the only place in DeGraff to buy a home-style meal. No one dared to open a competing eatery for fear it would die a painfully slow death of patronless starvation. In those days, some monopolies were good. Our family, however, seldom ate a meal that wasn't mom-prepared in our own kitchen. But when we did, Taylor's Restaurant was the treat of treats.

In addition to Becky's hot chocolate that I enjoyed on Saturdays at Taylor's, she also grilled amazing hamburgers long before Dave "Wendy's" Thomas from Columbus, Ohio, conceived his brilliantly-bunned beef patties. My guess is Dave was passing through DeGraff one pleasant day, decided to stop by Taylor's Restaurant for a hamburger lunch, and presto grease-o, his successful franchise was conceived. That's how good Becky Taylor's hamburgers were.

Wimpy Knight, who drove the school bus on DeGraff's rural routes, was a restaurant regular. He was a giant of a man who was liked by everybody, especially kids. Sometimes when I'd spend the weekend at Ned Heintz's farm, I'd get to ride Wimpy's bus to school with Ned on Monday morning, and that was a fun adventure for a city boy.

I suppose Wimpy had a real name, but I never heard it. Sam Hamsher dubbed him Wimpy after watching him eat two dozen White Castle hamburgers in a single sitting. Although White Castle hamburgers are junior-sized, the accomplishment was nonetheless an impressive feat. From that day on, he was known as Wimpy, sharing the name with Popeye's hamburger-inhaling friend.

DeGraff was also home to Howard "Turkey" Thompson, so nicknamed by his mother after he ate an entire twenty-pound turkey the Thanksgiving of his eighth-grade year. According to town lore, Turkey's mother was button-popping proud of her boy's appetite and the new handle she gave him (although the other family members were miffed after seeing their plates stacked low with Fuson's IGA ham loaf).

One fall Friday night after a home football game, Dad chauffeured all of us to Taylor's Restaurant for a post-game meal. As we squeezed into a front booth and began to scan the menu, I noticed Wimpy sitting at the busy counter with a plate of hamburgers in front of him. He hadn't started to eat and appeared to be ogling the herd for his first wrangle.

At that moment, Turkey Thompson, now a tenth grader, loudly entered the restaurant. Turkey spied Wimpy's mounded platter of burgers and trumpeted, "Hey, Wimpy, is that all you can eat? What's the deal, are you on a diet?" He bellowed a hearty, fat-guy laugh. "I guess you are wimpy! I eat more than that for a pre-snack snack. In fact, Mr. Hamburger Man, I'll bet I can eat more hamburgers than you."

Turkey's bantering got everyone's attention. The gauntlet was thrown down.

Before Wimpy could respond, Wig Taylor jumped in with a profitable proposal. "Tell you what, boys. Becky will cook all the hamburgers either one of you can eat. Whoever eats the most will be declared the winner. The deal is the loser pays for all hamburgers. What do you think? Do we have a contest?" Wig was a crafty one.

Without hesitation Wimpy and Turkey shook meat hooks, and Becky threw a slew of raw patties onto the grill. Wig removed the plate sitting patiently in front of Wimpy and announced he wanted each contestant to have a fresh start. All of the customers, including my family with Jeff lofted on Dad's shoulders and Mom cradling Kurt, began to crowd the counter to seek a better view. The Great Hamburger-Eating Contest in Taylor's Restaurant was about to commence.

But just before Becky finished the first batch of burgers, a noise squeaked from behind the crowd. It was the familiar, high-pitched voice of Frank Tully. Now, Frank Tully was an oddity of indefinable description. He looked like the character actor Joe Besser, who was a replacement Stooge toward the end of the Three Stooges' heyday, as well as the bratty "Stinky" of *Abbott and Costello* fame. In fact, Frank Tully looked more like Joe Besser than Stinky did.

No one knew for certain what Frank did for a living. The rumor was that his mother, with whom he'd lived his entire life, had come into a great deal of money and that after her death, Frank inherited it all. But that was only a rumor. No one knew for certain, not even Sam Hamsher.

What was known for certain was that Frank Tully never missed a civic event, a school event, a sports event, a church event, or even an insignificant event. Frank Tully defined ubiquitous. He was everywhere for everything within walking distance. I just assumed attendance was his occupation, like my dad's occupation was being a music teacher. An interview with Frank Tully by a *Bellefontaine*

Examiner reporter would have gone something like this.

"What do you do for a living, Mr. Tully?" Stretching to his full five-foot two-inch height with bald head sparkling, Frank Tully responds, "I attend, sir. I am an attendee, a professional attendee. I am in attendance."

So it was not unusual for Frank Tully to be somewhere among the crowd of people at Taylor's Restaurant that evening. What was unusual was for him to venture forth in such a bold manner. His helium-filled voice hovered above the crowd like a funny paper's cartoon caption before expanding, popping, and spilling words over us all.

"Mr. Taylor, can I eat hamburgers, too? Can I be in this contest?" Frank's words were met with absolute silence, and the only sound was the sizzling of Becky's patties frying on the grill. Bud Amos broke the spell.

"Let him in, Wig. Old Frank ain't gonna hurt nothin'. He's just a squirt." Laughter exploded as everyone looked to Wig for his answer.

"It's all right with me if it's okay with Wimpy and Turkey. What do you say, boys?"

Wimpy smiled. "Sure."

"Fine by me," Turkey said with a smirk.

"Agreed then," declared Wig. "The two losers foot the bill."

The crowd split so Frank could scamper through to the counter. Turkey flabbed over to the next stool, and Frank squeezed in between him and Wimpy. Looking at the three of them was a sight to behold, especially from behind the behinds. Wimpy and Turkey's big butts engulfed the counter stools like suction cups, while Frank's modest one perched him atop his stool. He looked like a toad wedged between two giant bullfrogs. The gluttonous trio of Turkey, Wimpy, and Shrimpy were ready to sing for their suppers.

By now, Becky had prepared several well-stacked layers

of hamburgers, and Wig slapped three burgers on each of three plates and slid them in front of the two gifted gastronomes and Frank. To wash the food down, Wimpy requested bottles of Coke, and Turkey demanded Dr. Pepper. Frank, the amateur of the three, simply wanted water. And with that, the contest was on.

Since it was a challenge of consumption and not speed, each one ate in his own unique style. Wimpy chomped around the hamburger circle-like, then popped the core into his mouth while reaching for the next one. Turkey ate greedily and ravenously, eyes shifting rapidly side-to-side like he was checking to be certain his food was safe from predators. Since Turkey Thompson came from a big family of big people of big eaters of big portions, his suspicious nature probably came naturally.

Frank was his usual odd wonderment. He ate his hamburgers like New England blue bloods nibble their watercress finger sandwiches during afternoon high tea— daintily yet deliberately.

Turkey began to fade after his third plate of three burgers and folded altogether during the fourth. He had underestimated the size of Becky's hamburgers. Suctioning off the stool, then tottering toward the front door with both hands clasped to his mouth, he gargled a good-bye and was not seen again for three weeks. Turkey later swore he didn't eat another hamburger until his junior year at Ohio State.

Wimpy looked strong until the seventh plate was set before him, while still having one hamburger left on the sixth. He surveyed the plate, glanced over toward Frank who was chewing dependably on his eighth hamburger, and stared back at his own plate. He then set the full plate in front of Frank.

"I'm stopping at seventeen, my little friend. Now I'm going to watch you bust trying to better that."

The remainder of The Great Hamburger-Eating Contest is committed to DeGraff folklore. It was almost 11:00 p.m. and the massive crowd had already thinned out. Dad said it was well past our bedtimes, and none of us argued with him. Jeff and Kurt had been sleeping for the past hour, Jeff in one of the booths and Kurt on Mom's lap, and I was fighting a losing battle against my eyelids. We slipped out the front door with several others.

Wig Taylor repeated his account of the final round and official results to congregated customers for months after. According to Wig, this was what happened, and John Kinnan and Elmer Morris, the only customers who were still there, verified his version.

At a little after midnight, Frank Tully ate his eighteenth hamburger to win the contest and then finished one more just because Becky had already prepared it, and he didn't want to seem impolite. Wimpy shook Frank's hand in sincere admiration and gave Wig four twenty-dollar bills for the whole works, including Turkey's share and a tip for Becky. He waddled out leaning on John and Elmer for support.

Wig also swears that right after Wimpy left the restaurant, Frank peered over the counter and, in an even higher-pitched voice, asked Becky, "You got any homemade apple pie back there? I've a taste for something sweet."

Chapter Ten

SWIMMING AT DEGRAFF'S CLUB MED

As a boy, I had several favorite places where I could disappear from one world and reappear in another. Loosely stretched down the hill behind our house, like the massive awning above Kinnan's Hardware, was Ernie's pasture field. Threading its way through it was the Bokenghelas Creek. The field and creek were my refuge, and Lady and I spent countless hours wading through both. In my adult life, I have looked for similar places for occasional hiding. I'm still looking.

Many small towns have secluded swimming holes, and DeGraff was no exception. We had The Stump, the Club Med of DeGraff. After the Bokenghelas Creek crawled through Ernie's pasture and under the Mill Street Bridge, it slithered for a couple of miles more before disappearing into thick brush and undergrowth. I'd lose track of it at that point and had no interest in following it farther, knowing my creek eventually lost its pulse to the Great Miami River.

Along the passable route downstream from the bridge and well out of sight from the road, however, the creek pooled suddenly and deeply into a perfect swimming hole below the stump of an old oak tree. Judging from the stump's massive girth, the tree must have been huge.

Rick D. Niece, Ph.D.

Our swimming spot could have been called The Pool as easily as it was The Stump, but for some reason it was always The Stump. We never knew who named it, why, or when. We just knew it had been used by generations of boys before us and hopefully would remain pure for the generations after. The Stump had no beach, just a bare dirt bank about twenty feet long and four or five feet wide. That was enough for us. No one wanted to sunbathe anyway when there was swimming to be done.

We swam in the deep middle of The Stump. Other than where the creek spread itself peanut butter thin on either side of the actual swimming hole, there were no shallow parts. We had to be careful when wading into the ankle-high water because the deep part was quietly waiting to surprise us. No one knew how deep The Stump actually was. I never touched bottom, and I don't know anyone else who did.

Bellefontaine had a wonderful, chlorinated pool at their City Park, equipped with two diving boards, a water slide, and an area for water basketball and volleyball. But the Bellefontaine pool also had lifeguards with shrill whistles and multiple rules printed in big red letters posted all around:

No RUNNING NEAR THE POOL
No PUSHING OTHERS INTO THE POOL
No BOTTLES AROUND THE POOL
No UNSUPERVISED CHILDREN IN THE POOL
No HORSEPLAY AROUND THE POOL
No DUNKING OTHERS IN THE POOL

Cripes, they might as well have had a sign that read: No fun in or around the pool during hours posted for swimming!

At The Stump, we had one unwritten rule, parent-enforced and kid-honored: "No swimming alone." That was it, and since the rule seemed like a good one, we obeyed it. I'm certain parents were a little concerned when their children said they were going swimming at The Stump and were relieved when their children came home safely. Over protection, however, never seemed to be an issue. My parents simply told me to be careful, and I always was.

The Stump was about as egalitarian as any place could be. In school, we had our special cliques of scholars, athletes, band, chorus, FFA, 4-H, and the gang of at-risk-to-dropout delinquents. My friends and I easily drifted in and out of most of these groups except the last one. Although those characters seemed okay, we usually avoided one another in school. At The Stump, it was different. At The Stump, everyone was accepted unconditionally. We were just a group of boys enjoying a swim.

The only time I actually got to know guys like Doc Manahan, Bill Greg, Chad and Brian Natham, and Ronnie Walker was at The Stump. Except for Doc, they weren't stellar students and usually seemed to be on or over the edge of trouble, seemingly spending as much time in the superintendent's office as in the classroom. According to Bill Greg during one of our man-to-boy Stump discussions, he was the smart one and not I.

"Why you want to be sittin' in class, twerp," he chided me, "when you can be sent to the superintendent's office and get a whiff of that hot Angle babe? Hell, I know she wants me."

And, hell, maybe Bill Greg was smarter than I gave him credit for. Marilyn Angle, the superintendent's secretary, was a definite babe. I was spending my school days with teachers like Mrs. Wammes, an excellent teacher but no Marilyn Angle. He had the Angle, and I had the "Wambat".

At The Stump, we talked a lot about girls—a whole lot

about girls. The funny thing is, I never saw a girl at The Stump, and none materialized no matter how much we fantasized. Maybe the tradition started out like a pirate ship rule where women were considered to be a curse and prohibited to go onboard. If they sneaked aboard, all kinds of disasters would befall the ship and crew. Maybe we were simply avoiding Stump disasters. Other than that, I don't know why we were womenless. Because The Stump was a secluded area, I suppose some guys took their girlfriends there after dark, but except for skinny-dipping, I doubt much swimming occurred.

I learned about sex at The Stump. Dad had given me a junior birds-and-bees lecture early in my young life, but his nervous descriptions were pretty much textbook and biologically oriented. The big guys' pantomimes and monologues were more graphic than Dad's examples.

Later in life, I discovered that Dad's accounts were more accurate but just not as interesting, while the big guys' purported deeds were fun to imagine but impossible to maneuver.

Harry Raymond "Doc" Manahan, Jr. was the wild man of The Stump Club Med. Doc was a smoker, and "Doc the Camel Man" was our full nickname for him in honor of his favorite brand of cigarettes. He was labeled Doc because among his crowd he was the studious one, but Doc the Camel Man fit him equally well.

Doc was the only one of us brave enough or indecent enough to swim completely naked. I can still picture Doc standing in the buff atop The Stump, four lit cigarettes stuffed in his mouth, and clapping to get our attention before cannon-balling into the water's belly while flapping like a dodo bird. He'd bob up quickly—smoking had given him the worst breath-holding capacity among us—four soggy cigarettes dangling limply from his lips.

The rest of us laughed at Doc like it was the first time we'd seen his stunt, and Doc would splash around pretending to puff his Camels while lapping up our laughter. He spent a lot of money on cigarettes, feeding his habit and keeping us entertained, but I'm certain he thought the cost was worth it. I know we did.

As a kid, I feared little at The Stump, though I suppose I should have feared more. The only things that made me nervous were the leeches and barbed channel catfish. But leeches were easily shriveled by sprinkling a little salt on them, and I never suffered the sting of a catfish barb although Charles Tamplin did once. I'm certain the channel cats were more afraid of us than we were of them.

None of us worried because The Stump didn't have lifeguards armed with whistles like they had at the artificial pool in Bellefontaine. We weren't concerned, because we carefully guarded one another and saved our whistles for Doc.

Rick D. Niece, Ph.D.

THEY WERE RONG

They were rong
my teachers were.
Said If I quit sckool.
droped out.
Id never make it in the "real" world.
Im dum I no,
cant spell or read to good.
I tried but gess I was just cut out
to be a yellow bird fourever.
And I never could figger out
how it felt to be a dafadil in spring
or why they cared each fall
how I spent last summer.
And grammer, well my comas,
just never seemed to fit to good.
And run ons.
But I did good inmath
and I can count good.
At least Mr. Hinkle thinks so
thats why he hired me at the Sinclair station.
I make change ok
so I gess Im doin alright.
and I told Miss McGee my old English teacher
so when she stoped the other day for gas.
I just told her how this hear at the station
made more cents then all that other stuff.
and I think she believed me to
cause she didn't laff or nothing,
she just shook her head
and sorta cleared her throte.

CHAPTER ELEVEN

RINGERS

His given name was Cleo, but in high school my Grandpa claimed the new name of Jack, after the boxer Jack Dempsey. When his parents asked why he changed his name, the budding pugilist answered, "Name one boxer named Cleo." Hearing no argument, he was Jack from that moment on.

Grandpa Jack loved boxing. Although I have never been an avid fan of the sport, I do remember watching Friday night fights on the *Gillette Cavalcade of Sports* with him. He could explain better than the commentators the specific strategies each boxer used and was able to predict, almost to the point, how the three judges were going to score a bout.

As a young man, Grandpa Jack boxed as a welterweight but never competed professionally or even semi-pro. A Golden Gloves program didn't exist in Lima during his prime, so he'd go to the downtown YMCA, work out with a local trainer, and box real rounds a couple of times a week against limited talent.

A tarnished silver trophy with a boxer in the classic stance sat on the end table beside his easy chair. Grandpa Jack won the trophy by making it to the finals of a military tournament when he was in the Army, but he lost the championship match on a split decision and still complained, decades later, that he was robbed.

The trophy nameplate read:

**RUNNER UP
WELTERWEIGHT CLASS
JACK "THE RINGER" GEYER**

I once asked why he was called The Ringer, and he told me it was because when he wasn't on duty, he was usually in the camp's boxing ring working on his style. Then Grandpa Jack smiled, tapped me playfully on the chin with a soft right uppercut, and bragged, "Besides that, when The Ringer tagged his opponent, the guy heard ringing in his ears worse than Quasimodo."

I remember two distinct photographs of Grandpa Jack. In one, he is posing as a boxer, the only time I ever saw him without a shirt. He had a wiry, lithe, athletic build and swore his physique came naturally, because he never lifted weights or did serious workouts.

In the other photograph, taken in November of 1917 at Camp Sherman in Montgomery, Alabama, he is in his Army uniform standing among the other infantrymen in the 37th Division. Grandpa Jack served in World War I with the 111th Supply Train. He'd never talk about the war, not even when I was doing a research paper in high school. The assignment was to interview a relative who had served in World War I or World War II, and I telephoned to ask about his experiences as a foot soldier. He said no. At first, I thought he was teasing me, but quickly realized he was dead serious. He explained he had vowed never to relive the war and was not going to begin now, not even for me. I interviewed my father instead.

My brother Jeff has the picture of Grandpa Jack and his Army division hanging on a den wall. When I asked Jeff how he got it, he said he'd asked for it when he was helping my grandparents pack for their move back to Indiana. I'm glad he did. After Grandpa Jack's death and then my Grandma Ruth's a few years later, the relatives who lived close to them scavenged their possessions before the rest of us arrived. Not much was left to choose from, and I ended up with nothing, not even his tarnished trophy.

Grandpa Jack worked for a large oil refinery in Lima. When we'd drive for a visit and enter the city limits, I could see the refinery's towering smoke stack with a flame shooting out of it. Grandpa Jack tested the oil's purity in an area beneath that flaming stack. I was proud to think he had such an important responsibility.

One evening during supper, my Uncle Richard called to tell us Grandpa Jack had suffered a serious heart attack while splitting firewood. Mom and Dad drove right away to Lima and didn't return until late the next day. Grandpa survived, but the attack weakened his heart so much he could never do anything strenuous again and was forced to go on permanent disability. That was a major lifestyle change for him and my grandmother. He had, in the skip of a heartbeat, gone from an active, vibrant man to an inactive, sedate one.

The year after his heart attack, Grandma Ruth suggested they move back to Indiana to be closer to the children and grandchildren of her first marriage. Because of that move, our visits unfortunately became less frequent. I missed them.

In Swayzee, Indiana, his life activities were reduced to simple routines. He'd rise early, eat a light breakfast, read the local and state newspapers front to back and then back to front, after which he'd take a nap until lunch. After lunch, he'd drive downtown, flock with a group of newly found World War I buddies, and roost with them on a couple of large black, wrought iron benches in front of the drugstore until returning home for supper. After supper, Grandma Ruth knitted while Grandpa Jack slept in his easy chair, the television on but entertaining neither. The cycle rewound itself again and again and again.

The downtown time with his friends was a daily highlight, and I think the conversations are what kept him going for so long after his first heart attack. The benches were known throughout Swayzee as the "Liars' Benches." Grandpa Jack said the name was appropriate, adding that no one should believe much of what was said by any of them sitting there. Veracity, I'm sure, was sprinkled sparingly throughout the endlessly respun yarns. I quickly gathered the point was never to let truth get in the way of a good story.

During our visits to Swayzee, Grandpa Jack sometimes let me tag along downtown with him. The first time I went I met Dusty Rhoades, the loudest of the liars flock. Grandpa Jack talked a lot about Dusty Rhoades and seemed to admire him. But to me old Dusty looked pretty much like the tail end of a misspent life.

Before we even shook hands, Dusty asked me, in a menacingly loud voice, how it felt to be a grandson of the former welterweight champion of the Midwest. I didn't flinch at the size of the whopper Grandpa Jack had obviously concocted for Dusty and his bench mates. I suspect Dusty was testing my loyalty as much as Grandpa Jack's truthfulness. Even at that young age, I knew family blood was thicker than the tedium of watered-down truth.

Their tall tale spinning was as contagious as chicken pox because I came down with a quick case of spin-itis. With improvised, fast-action animation, I demonstrated to Dusty and the crew how Grandpa Jack taught me to set up a right-fisted uppercut knockout punch after a combination of sharp, piston-like left-hand jabs. I finished the story in a flurry of pugilistic prevarications and the boastful declaration that my sequence of moves was how Jack "The Ringer" Geyer knocked out Raymond "The Skipper" Ceylor for the welterweight title of the Midwest. Whew, what a whopper! Skip Ceylor was a classmate of mine whose name just popped into my inventive little head.

After my performance, I reached out to Dusty Rhoades, shook his hand, and courageously declared, "Glad to meet you, Dusty. Want to go a few rounds?" Dusty slapped me enthusiastically on the back and announced, "Men, clear some room for this little guy. We got ourselves a liar in training." I squeezed in between Grandpa Jack and a hard-of-hearing cigar smoker named Fat Petey, satisfied that The Ringer's reputation was intact for at least one more card.

Bernie Jones was always thinking. I guess that's what happens when you sit in a wheelchair all day with nothing else to do. I could tell when Bernie had a brainstorm because as I sped down the hill toward his house to deliver the newspaper, his shouts to me would be an octave higher than usual.

"Hurry up, Rickie, my boy, hurry up! Got an idea today!"

I'd pedal faster so I could make a dramatic gravel-spraying stop a couple of feet in front of his chair. His ideas were usually impractical strokes of unimaginable invention, but I'd listen carefully anyway before dashing his hopes as gently as possible. After all, he'd waited all day to tell me. In most cases, my ears were open, but my mind was mostly closed.

"What's the new idea this time, Bernie? What's going on in that head of yours?" I tapped lightly on his head and asked, "What's the abbreviation for mountain, Bernie?"

"Yeah, Rickie, it's M-T—empty—and you pulled that one on me a hundred times already. C'mon, I'm serious now."

I could tease Bernie only so much. He needed someone to take him seriously, and most days I was his only willing candidate.

"You and your family play horseshoes, right?"

Where was this going?

"Yeah, Bernie, we have a set, why?"

"This Saturday after you deliver the papers, come back with the horseshoes and teach me to play."

Wait, whoa! The visual image of Bernie pitching a horseshoe was way beyond even my wildest imagination. I mentally pictured a galloping horse throwing a shoe with more accuracy than Bernie could pitch one. But I kindly kept that spectacle to myself.

"Geez, Bernie, I don't know. I'd have to carry the horseshoes and the steel stakes over here on my bike, and I'd need a sledgehammer to whack the stakes into the ground. I don't think it'll work."

Sometimes you could successfully discourage Bernie and other times you couldn't budge him with a forklift. This was a no-budger time.

"Come on, Rickie, please! My dad has a sledgehammer. Teach me horseshoes. Come on, Rickie, please!"

How do you say no to a wheelchair-bound guy with cerebral palsy? His idea was flimsier than a Three Stooges two-reel plot, but who was I to tell him it was goofy.

"Sure, Bernie, sounds like fun. We've got ourselves a date for horseshoes this Saturday."

That was on Monday, and each day I delivered the paper during the rest of the week, I had an excuse made up for canceling our Saturday plans. And each day Bernie greeted me with something like, "Three more days, Rickie, my boy, three more days to horseshoes."

The clincher was Saturday afternoon when I delivered the paper, and he was wearing a brown cotton glove on his right hand.

"Okay, Bernie, I'll bite. Why the glove?"

Bernie flashed his yellow teeth. "Rickie, my boy, I decided this will be my throwing hand. Mom says you got to be careful handling horseshoes. I'm protecting myself."

I had never considered if Bernie was right- or left-handed, and I doubt he knew for certain himself, but the gloved hand made him an official right-hander. As I prepared to open the paper and give Bernie his daily *Dick Tracy*, the gloved hand shooed me away.

"Just keep pedaling, Rickie, my boy. No time to waste. Big horseshoe match at the Jones house tonight!"

I finished the route and had a quick supper with my family. Dad helped me pack the four horseshoes and two metal stakes into his old Navy garment sack, making the load no more difficult than my regular newspaper bag, although it clanked more going over the railroad tracks. Bernie was waiting for me, a sledgehammer by his chair.

"I figure we have a couple of hours before dark, Bernie. I'll explain the rules while I set the stuff up."

I didn't know all of the official rules for horseshoe pitching, but rules weren't too important for this match. Bernie only had to know the basics. I explained that a ringer is worth three points, and if no one throws a ringer, the shoe closest to the post counts for one point. That was about all I knew. As I was hammering the stakes and yammering about the scoring, Bernie interrupted me.

"You're wasting time. Three points for a ringer, and one point for getting close. What are we waiting for?"

I pulled his chair beside the near post, and as we looked at the second post about ten yards away, I knew the moment of truth had arrived. How was Bernie going to hold a horseshoe, let alone pitch it? Bernie looked at me, and I looked at Bernie. We spent several long seconds looking at one another. I gave in first.

"Okay, Bernie, tell you what. For the first game, I'll help you hold the horseshoe. You and I will swing your arm together until you master the technique." He agreed.

For his first game of horseshoes, I did most of the holding and throwing for him. Gradually, he was able to gain a grip around the horseshoe, but he/we never came close to a post. After our shared throws, I'd pitch my own, and then wheel him to the opposite post. Back and forth we played, wheeling and walking, talking and laughing.

Twenty-one points wins the match, and I skunked Bernie twenty-one to nothing the first game. I really did try everything in my power to keep the score down and to get him some points. I threw left-handed. I closed my eyes. I even pitched behind my back show-off style, but I wasn't showing off. I just didn't want Bernie to feel humiliated. But fat chance of that happening, because he was having the time of his life. Just before the second game, Bernie declared his independence.

"This game I throw the shoe myself. You help get it in my hand, but I do the rest."

"Oh, brother," I mumbled to myself, half-hoping Bernie would hear my doubts.

I helped Bernie with his grip and moved behind him and to the left, satisfied I'd found a horseshoe safety zone. Silly me. Bernie wound up in his herky-jerky motion and the horseshoe released. I still have a crescent-shaped scar and slight bump on my shin, just above the right ankle, where the horseshoe thudded then ringed my foot.

"Dammit, Bernie!" I blurted without thinking. I had never sworn at him before, and the second the words slipped out of my mouth, I was sorry. But doggone it, that hurt! Bernie cranked his head back and looked at the horseshoe ringing my foot.

"I don't suppose your leg counts as a ringer, does it, Rickie, my boy?" Even through the pain of a throbbing shin, I couldn't help but laugh.

"No, Bernie, I can't give you any points for that one. Nice try though."

Our second and third games also ended in skunks, and sunset was upon us. "Bernie, I need to get home before it's completely dark."

Bernie would hear none of it. "Rickie, my boy, you have a light on your bike. We still have time."

He was right. It wasn't as if DeGraff was a dangerous traffic town, even at night. The last bike versus car accident occurred in broad daylight a few years before when Tobias "Wiggy" Wiggleson, who rode his bike around town daily, ran into the back of Lafe Funk's pickup truck that was double-parked illegally in front of the post office. Wounded Wiggy limped into the post office and demanded that Auggie Leagre, the postmaster, drive him to Dr. Blank's office in the mail truck with yellow lights flashing. Auggie claimed he was too busy and told Lafe, who was waiting in line to buy stamps, to take care of Wiggy himself. Humiliated, Wiggy ended up being transported to the doctor in the back of the pickup truck that "caused" the assault in the first place, his banged-up bicycle bouncing beside him. Both survived.

"Okay, Bernie, just one more game, then I need to go."

Halfway into the match, we were both having trouble seeing either post through the vanishing light. Finally, it was impossible to see a post directly in front of us, and the time to end our evening had come.

"One last throw, Bernie, and that's it." I gripped the shoe

in his hand, and after feeling him tighten around it, I moved far to the right.

He twice swung his arm backward and forward in a labored arc before letting go of the horseshoe. Neither of us actually saw its flight. And then came the most magical of sounds—metal hitting metal. Bernie gasped. I gasped.

I ran to the post and leaned down, looking and feeling at the same time. It wasn't a ringer. I could feel the rounded part of the horseshoe several inches from the post where it had struck and bounced back. I flipped the horseshoe quickly to collar it around the post.

"Rickie, is it a ringer? Is it a ringer?"

I hurried back and wheeled Bernie to the post. "Bernie, it's a ringer! You got a ringer! Your pitch was perfect, buddy, the best of the evening."

He was squinting his eyes and trying to see the horseshoe circling the post. I grabbed his hand, and reaching down with his gloved hand in mine, we touched the ringed horseshoe together and captured his moment.

After packing the shoes and posts back into the Navy sack, I wheeled Bernie to his front door.

"See you Monday, Bernie."

"See you Monday, Rickie, my boy." He paused a Bernie pause. "You know what? We don't have to play horseshoes anymore. I'm too good for you now."

I smiled at him. "Yeah, Bernie, you're too good for me now. See you Monday."

I whistled all the way home, but kept an eye out for Lafe Funk's truck.

CHAPTER TWELEVE

AN ACT OF COMFORT

I was genuinely awed by the eccentric diversity of my newspaper customers. From delightful to interesting to unique, I grew to cherish them all. I tried not to show favoritism but with Bernie, Fern, and Miss Lizzie, I did have favorites. Close to the top of that list was Mrs. Mary Waite.

Mary Waite and her husband Bryan lived in a modest, one-story house situated in the middle of a well-manicured acre of Kentucky bluegrass and surrounded by rosebushes and a labyrinth of hedges. In his day, Mr. Waite was famous around DeGraff for being a precisionist about his lawn and landscaping. My guess is he'd be diagnosed today as obsessive compulsive.

He was also the town's best furniture refurbisher. No chair or couch was yard sale bound or beyond repair if it found its way into his expert hands. In all the years I delivered the paper, I never actually saw him in their house. He was either trimming the bushes to ornate perfection or busy in his workshop that was connected to their house by a pea gravel pathway. My mother's favorite chair once found its way down that path and into his workshop.

During a summer Sunday visit to my Uncle Ude's farmhouse when I was five or six, my mother rediscovered an antique Queen Anne chair she remembered from her childhood. The chair was languishing in Uncle Ude's attic-like storage space of a living room. She asked if she could have it, and Uncle Ude, always the generous man, gave it to her without hesitation.

I loved afternoons at my Uncle Ude's homestead because he and his house were wonderfully unkempt, a veritable roof-covered pigsty with occasional running water and almost bearable smells. I remember my mother once looking at a pile of dirty plates on the kitchen table and mockingly asking, "Ulys, do you ever put a dish away?"

He smiled his single-tooth smile and answered, "Sure I do, Dortha Jean. Every time one of the cats licks a plate clean, I know it's ready for the cabinet."

The Queen Anne chair was serving as the resting place for a stack of well-worn *National Geographic* magazines, at least two decades of post-World War I calendars, and a tattered Chinese checkers box stuffed with acorns. Uncle Ude scooped all these into a large tin washtub that was already half-filled with corncobs and doorknobs and then hauled the Queen Anne to our car. I swear I heard the squeal of a cat as he emptied the chair's contents into the washtub, but I never actually saw it.

Mom delivered the chair, pretty much on its last Queen Anne legs, to Bryan Waite, and he worked his magic. He restored the chair to rose-petal newness, transforming it into what became the showcase of my parent's various living rooms for years to come. Bryan Waite was DeGraff's Rodin of both wood and verdure.

His wife Mary was an invalid. The first couple of years I delivered papers to them, I thought her condition was a treatable sickness, curable with proper medications and hearty helpings of homemade soup. I didn't understand why she never got better, so one time I asked Dr. Blank, DeGraff's only medical doctor and general practitioner, about her. He patiently explained that invalids like Mrs. Waite rarely improved. The best medical prescription, he said, was to make them feel as comfortable as possible. I wanted to help however I could.

As it turned out, I was able to do something. Mrs. Waite made one simple, albeit unusual, request of me. She wanted me to read *The Bellefontaine Examiner* obituaries to her. Since Bernie Jones and *Dick Tracy* were the only other members on my oral interpretation list, I figured I could easily accommodate Mrs. Waite. She explained that her husband never read the obituary section, and she got depressed reading the obituaries alone. I decided if my reading a few obituaries made her feel comfortable, that was the least I could do. Fortunately, she wasn't interested in the entire column, just the name, date and place of birth, and survivors.

I didn't read every day for Mrs. Waite as I did for Bernie. I found my cue to be where she was located when I delivered the paper. If she was sitting outside and bonneted by the rose trellis her husband had built for her, it was a reading day. If she was waiting in a chair just inside the opened front door, it was a reading day. In other words, when she was visible, I knew she was having a good day and would be up for hearing the obituaries. On days I delivered the paper and she was nowhere in sight, she was having a bad day. Bryan Waite once explained to me, while pruning the roses on the trellis, that on his wife's bad days, the obituaries were too real for her.

Because Mrs. Waite took comfort in obituaries, I never felt morbid while reading them. Although she was an invalid—I never once saw her walk or even stand upright— she found something to be cheerful about with each obituary. If the person who died was older than she was, Mrs. Waite would smile and say, "I'm going to live to be older than that." If the deceased was younger than she, her response was, "I've already outlived that one!" Ironically, it turned out, the obituaries seemed to give her something to live for.

Children's obituaries, however, were the exception to our reading rule, and the few I read made her sad. She'd whisper, "That is not right. That is just not right." I'd stop, carefully refold the paper, and place it gently on her lap before quietly leaving. When I finally came to realize the obituaries of children upset her, I stopped reading them altogether. Although she never said anything to me, I suspect she was, after a time, on to my omissions. Children died, even in DeGraff.

Toward the end of my sophomore year in high school, Mrs. Waite's bad days began to outnumber her good ones. Our conversations were briefer now, with me carrying the bulk of the talk. I saw her very few times that spring and summer. The last time I read to her was in early September when the trellised roses in full bloom still surrounded her.

Mrs. Waite died one spring-like late October afternoon, unusually nice weather for that time of year in Ohio. The next evening in the quiet of my bedroom, I slowly unfolded *The Bellefontaine Examiner* and read her obituary softly aloud to myself:

Mary Ellen Sawyer Waite, born in 1902, is survived by husband Bryan. One daughter, Susan Elizabeth, died shortly after birth. Mrs. Waite was a lifelong resident of DeGraff and will be buried in Greenwood Cemetery.

I found comfort in the reading.

A Complex Cycle In Simple Terms

Born
Weaned
Crawl, Walk, Talk
"Mommy," "Daddy"
Getting bigger
Growing up

Leave home
Off to school
New friends
Study
Graduation

"Hello, World"
Job Success
Courtship
"I love you"
Marriage
Children
Raise them
Teach them
Watch them grow
Empty nest
Adjustments
"I love you"

Grandchildren
Hold them
Show them
Watch them grow
Retire
She dies.
Sadness
Alone
He dies.
Buried and gone

That quick
That complex
That simple
That's life

CHAPTER THIRTEEN

WATCHING OVER FROM ABOVE

Thunderstorms can blow up quickly in Ohio. A day turns hot and muggy, a few clouds congregate, caress each other for a moment, and then procreate by melting into one all-consuming, dark-roofed cloud. And then BOOM! A rainstorm and lightning show ensues with thunderous surround sound.

One summer August day, several weeks before the start of a new school year, I'd ridden my bike to Hougen's garage to fold the newspapers. The sun was shining when I started out, but rain began pouring before I could begin the route. The thunder kettle-drummed and lightning stabbed downward. John Slater, the Tamplin brothers, and I glanced nervously at each other as we watched the rain from inside the safety of the garage.

Each Christmas, the fine folks at *The Bellefontaine Examiner* gave their carriers new waterproofed canvas bags as a gift for us to tote around their papers. The canvas bag had a flap to pull over the opening for the papers, and both sides of the bag had ***THE BELLEFONTAINE EXAMINER*** stenciled in big bold blue letters. I figured all the free advertising I did for the paper, biking around DeGraff six days a week like a mobile billboard, should have been worth at least an extra buck or two, but what did I know? I was only a kid who annually wore out his canvas bag and was gifted a new one at Christmas. On this inclement August day, the waterproofed, flap-covered canvas bag was perfect for delivering papers, and I was grateful. I'd get soaked, but my freight would stay snug and bone-dry.

After we finished folding the papers, Charles and Herb decided to wait out the storm in the garage. Being the more adventuresome or foolhardy of the group, John and I decided we couldn't wait any longer hoping for the weather to break. The papers needed to be delivered. So off we sloshed into the storm, dragon tails of water sprouting behind our bike tires. Lady was with me. She loved the rain, although she wasn't too crazy about the thunder and lightning, and she ran beside me head up and tonguing the drops.

Delivering papers in the rain was one of my two least favorite activities. Delivering them on below-zero afternoons was the other. But being cold and wet was a natural way of life for us paper carriers.

Because of the driving rain, I couldn't just pitch the papers onto the porches as I usually did. Instead, I had to stop at each house and place the paper behind the screen door. Some customers even encouraged me to open their unlocked front doors and drop the paper inside. (I saw some interesting sights during several of those unexpected door openings, but they shall remain private.)

The storm was torrential, and I was running way behind my regular schedule. Thoroughly soaked, I decided there was nothing I could do except to keep pedaling and finish the route as quickly as possible. Luckily, I wasn't afraid of lightning, because hurled bolts were searing the sky from every direction.

As I skimmed toward the box factory, I thought I heard something through the thunder and pelting rain but wasn't certain. The sound was like the noise a large animal makes when it's been hurt. When I heard it again and then once more, I knew the source. Bernie!

"Help! Help!"

"My God!" was all I could think, as I sliced my way through the rain. "What is Bernie doing out in this storm?"

As I passed the box factory and just before I cleared the railroad tracks, a flash of lightning lit the entire sky to the west, and I could see Bernie in his chair in his side yard, framed against the white of his house like some gothic painting in an Alfred Hitchcock movie. I felt sick to my stomach. "What's going on here? What's going on?" I fumed aloud while racing faster. "This is crazy!" Bernie in his metal wheelchair, rain pouring down, lightning flashing all around—what was going on?

As soon as I reached his house, I dumped my bike and papers in one motion and rushed up behind him. Bernie stared at me silently with a look that seemed to say, "Where have you been?" I pushed at his chair in a panic but my feet slipped, slamming my chin against one of the chair's metal handles. I got better traction and began pushing Bernie to the front door as fast as I could manage. The door was closed, but the small overhang above it gave us some protection. Lady shook herself, and the excess water created a pint-sized rainstorm before she flopped down next to us.

"Bernie, what's going on? Where are your parents?" It was August, yet Bernie was extremely pale and his yellow teeth chattered a dead-of-winter chatter. He was too scared and saturated to speak.

I pushed the front door of his house open and pulled Bernie inside. In all the time I'd known Bernie and delivered the paper, I had never been inside his house. I'd seen the kitchen from the doorway before, but I'd never been invited inside.

The kitchen was small with yellowed linoleum flooring and daisy-flowered wallpaper. Everything looked bright and surprisingly cheery except for the dark cabinets that had even darker round knobs. The kitchen table had two chairs and an open space large enough for Bernie's chair. A dish towel was folded neatly on the countertop, and everything was in its place with no dishes in the sink. Who knows why you notice what you notice, especially during such dreadful times, but I vividly remember every detail of that kitchen.

I looked at Bernie to see if he was responding any better. He wasn't. Water continued to drip down his face from his soaked baseball cap. I couldn't distinguish the rainwater from what I suspect were tears. He looked so helpless and humiliated. I was angry.

"Where are your parents, Bernie?" I pried the cap from his head, pitched it into the sink, and grabbed the dish towel to begin wiping his face and head. Still no answer.

"Bernie, I need a bigger towel, several towels. Where are they?" He jerked his head forward, and I saw a hallway and hurried over toward the first opened door. It was the bathroom, and I snatched three towels from a rack beside an old-fashioned freestanding bathtub. I massaged Bernie's head with one of the towels, determined to get at least part of him dry. After a minute or two, I changed towels and began again until his hair was only slightly damp.

"We've got to get you out of these clothes, Bernie," I said while pulling the white T-shirt pasted to his body up and over his head, then drying his back, arms, and chest. I was trying to figure out how to remove his soaking wet pants when I noticed a line of plastic tubing stretched near his waist and disappearing down into the side of his pants above the belt.

I hadn't thought much about it before, but in those seconds I suddenly began to realize the daily struggles with which Bernie dealt, struggles I could barely imagine. I didn't know how any of it worked for him, but I correctly guessed functions routine for the rest of us were diffcult for Bernie, and I didn't want to intrude upon his private life any further. He'd had enough humiliation for one day. I did my best to drape a dry towel over his shoulders, trying to cover his chest and give him warmth.

"I think we'd better keep your pants on, buddy, but let me take your shoes and socks off." I untied the laces, pulled off the shoes, and peeled away his socks. I dried his feet as best I could, then pressed the towel against his legs and lap, trying to sponge away the remaining wetness.

"Bernie, I wish they made a giant squeegee for humans. Up your front, down your back, zip, zip, zip. You'd be dry as a bone!" He still gave me no reaction.

I figured we needed some humor. "Come on, Bernie, you have to start responding." I then leaned into his face, raised my voice, and demanded, "Are you all right?" He nodded a slight yes. "No, Bernie," I corrected him. "You cannot be all right because half of you is left." I knew the joke was cornier than any of Flippo the Clown's lame lines, but I was getting desperate.

He managed a weak smile, and I finally felt some relief. Bernie was back. But just as suddenly, he looked panicked again.

"Rickie, you're bleeding! Your chin!"

I reached up, and sure enough I was bleeding and had actually bled quite a bit. The front of my shirt was sticky red and my chin felt syrupy. I looked like a messy little kid who'd chomped his way through a cinnamon red candy apple at the county fair. I went to the sink and dabbed myself with cold water. "Yeeow, that stings!" I didn't want to ruin a towel, so I packed a handful of napkins from the kitchen table against my throbbing chin.

I realized I must have ripped the bottom of my chin when I slipped and hit Bernie's wheelchair, but in all the excitement nothing hurt until now. And now it really hurt. I felt dizzy and queasy from seeing my own blood, so I crumpled down to the floor by Bernie's bare feet. Had I been alone I would have cried, but not in front of Bernie. He'd been brave, and I wanted to be, too.

I clicked into slow motion as I sat on the linoleum floor, chin throbbing, and Bernie looking down at me. The throbbing was keeping time with my heartbeat, and I closed my eyes.

The front door suddenly banged open, and Bernie's mom and dad rushed into the kitchen.

"Bernie!" his mother said, anguished. "Oh, Bernie, we are sorry. We are so sorry." She looked at me and saw the bloody napkins matted to my chin. "Rickie, you're hurt!"

"I'm okay, Mrs. Jones, really I am. Take care of Bernie."

Bernie's dad didn't say anything, but I could tell he was surveying the situation, trying to figure out what the chain of events had been. After a moment, he spoke. "We had an emergency and had to leave in a hurry for Bellefontaine. No time to ask anyone to look after Bernie, but we thought he'd be okay. Damn rainstorm! The main road was flooded driving home, and we took a back road. Damn rainstorm!" Bernie's dad was a no-nonsense man, and this was difficult for him.

Glancing apologetically toward his wife and then to Bernie, he confessed, "She didn't want to leave Bernie by himself, but I insisted he'd be fine." He paused to breathe an extended breath. "I'm sorry this happened." His eyes shifted slowly to me. "Thanks, son."

I was no longer angry with either of them. Bernie's mom

and dad looked ashamed, but I didn't know what to say to make them feel better. Nothing seemed right. I looked outside, and the rain had let up to a mist-like drizzle. "I'd better go. I still have the rest of my route to finish." I patted Bernie on the arm and walked outside to my bike while they both attended to him.

It was then that I saw the most horrible sight of an already horrid day. When I dropped my bike and newspaper bag in my haste to help Bernie, the newspapers had spilled out and scattered like pick-up sticks. They were all waterlogged.

As I tried to stuff them back into the bag, I remembered I hadn't given a paper to Bernie or his parents. I grabbed one, ran back to the house, and handed Mr. Jones his dripping stick of ruined newspaper.

Then I started to cry, an uncontrollable sobbing cry. The pent-up dam burst, and I flooded over. I was bawling.

"Come with me, son," Mr. Jones said, leading me out the front door. "I'm taking you home." I didn't protest.

Mr. Jones carefully laid my bike in the back of his pickup truck, gathered the soggy papers into the bag, and placed them on the floor in front of me. Lady jumped into the bed of the truck at his first command. I was gulping down little sobs, and we didn't speak during the drive.

The sun broke through the mist, and I caught sight of a rare double rainbow curving through the emerging blue sky beyond our house. I nudged Mr. Jones, and he looked and smiled down at me.

Mom and Dad came to the porch when they saw us pull into the driveway, but I stayed in the truck while Mr. Jones got out and spoke to them. I don't know why I stayed in his truck, but it felt safe. Finally, Dad opened the door and helped me out, rubbing my head like a puppy's. Mom looked at my chin and sucked air through her teeth but stayed calm. They thanked Mr. Jones, and he left without saying anything else.

Mom drove me to Dr. Blank's office, and he cleaned the wound and sewed in eighteen stitches. I still have crisscross scars on my chin. Dad and Jeff finished my route, taking the papers to each customer and explaining what had happened. Dad later told me that most of my customers weren't too upset, and I remember hoping there wasn't much important news happening in the world or Logan County in that edition.

Mr. and Mrs. Jones never mentioned the incident to me, and Bernie and I didn't talk about it either. Some adventures aren't fun to relive.

But after that day, every time I collected for a week with a holiday in it, Mr. Jones gave me the extra nickel. I took it gratefully and stuffed it in my left front pocket with the others.

LONG AGO

I once, long ago, heard grass
sigh and sing
as it furled in the wind.
I saw it spring with rain
and wave to clouds.
And I would cry when green turned brown
and living turned withered
and ground turned barren.
But that was long ago.

I once, long ago, sat nose to nose with flowers
and smelled their glory
and stroked their plumage
and rubbed their pollen
and laughed aloud back to them.
And I would cry when, one by one,
they stripped bare and slouched,
nude heads downward.
But that was long ago.

I once, long ago, made friends with trees
and rode them piggyback
and borrowed their arms for slingshots and bows.
I sat by their feet and heard their stories,
and they listened to mine.
And I would cry when green turned brown
and arms turned bare
and trees turned silent.
But that was long ago.

Rick D. Niece, Ph.D.

Long, long ago
in a simple childhood world
of grass and flowers and trees.

Now,
I sometimes stand by my window
and watch the rain
and wish I could cry.

CHAPTER FOURTEEN

MEN OF GOOD HUMOR

During our early years in DeGraff, my father directed the choirs in several different Protestant churches. As a family, we were faithful church attendees, although the particular church we attended was seldom consistent one year to the next. When I was in the sixth grade, however, the DeGraff Methodist Church became our permanent place of worship.

The basement of the Methodist Church was used to host a variety of functions, and among my favorites were the potluck dinners after church and the evening suppers before special programs. Each church woman had her specialty dish, and to this day I can still taste my buffet-line choices: my mother's baked beans, Goose Roby's shredded chicken sandwiches, Mag Comer's sugar-cured ham and candied yams, Suzie Heintz's German potato salad, Frances Tamplin's fudge-layered chocolate cake, Nannette Wren's graham cracker pudding, and Jinny Knief's double custard cream pie. Cruise ship cuisine is not their equal.

The Cub Scouts and Boy Scouts held their weekly meetings in the church basement. Jeff and I were scouts, and I'm certain Jeff still shares a record with Bob Smithers for the longest sustained laugh during a formal Cub Scout induction ceremony.

Bob Smithers, one of the high school science teachers,

served as scoutmaster for our Cub Scout and Boy Scout troops. He was a stickler for formality, especially during solemn ceremonies. The year Jeff was inducted, Bob decided having each young scout recite a line of the official Scout Pledge would be more impressive than the scoutmaster reading the whole thing himself. Each inductee was to memorize an individual line and then repeat it as he lit a smaller candle from the larger "Source of Truth and Light" candle.

Jeff was assigned the last line, "… and Cub Scouts prepares us for adulthood." The line was simple, and Jeff had no problem memorizing it. For the entire week leading up to the ceremony, Jeff cleverly incorporated the line into his bedtime prayers, giving him extra practice and some heavenly insurance. With one line and lots of practice, we figured there was no way Jeff could mess it up. We were all far too optimistic.

Dad was seated in the front row poised with our box-shaped Brownie Hawkeye Camera ready to snap a picture of Jeff's big moment. As Jeff lit his candle, he smiled proudly at Dad and delivered his line, "…and Cub Scouts prepares us for adultery."

Jeff and the other innocent Cub Scouts had no idea why his words were met with gales of laughter. I couldn't believe my ears, Mom smothered her face, and Dad was shaking with a convulsive horselaugh I'd never heard erupt from him before, causing him to flash a perfect picture of his left foot.

After a couple of minutes, the laughter still had not subsided and tears continued to cascade down the faces of the adults. Bob Smithers, seeing his well-planned candlelight ceremony going up in flames, stood and waved his arms as if to plead for some semblance of decorum.

After we quieted to a few restrained titters, Bob

delivered the coup de grace. "Well, friends, if Cub Scouts prepares these lads for adultery, one can only imagine what's in store for our Boy Scouts."

More laughter exploded and a new comedy team of Bob Abbott and Jeff Costello was the talk of the town throughout the following weeks. Jeff, God bless him, still got his Cub Scout pin and eventually became a Boy Scout troop leader. I cannot attest to his fidelity in later years.

My youngest brother Kurt also had his moment of glory during a program in the Methodist Church basement. One Wednesday evening, the elementary Sunday school classes performed a dramatization of several parables from the Bible. In one of the scenes, Kurt played the role of a sandal maker. After two king-sized sheets used for curtains were pulled apart along a clothesline extended wall to wall, Kurt and a couple of other "sandal makers" could be seen sitting on a long bench and cobbling with wooden mallets. Kurt didn't have any lines, so my family and I had no reason to be nervous.

At events like this, the majority of the audience members were parents and other family members. Giving up the prime part of a Wednesday evening was serious business in DeGraff. A few other church members usually attended as a courtesy, but most of us had a relative on the portable wooden stage. Jeff and I were in attendance out of enforced familial loyalty and not because we were overly excited to watch Kurt and the other amateur squirts perform.

Seated in the middle of the front row of folding metal chairs, elbows on his knees and with his chin in his hands, was Frank Tully. Frank, as I mentioned, seldom missed any type of social event in DeGraff, and he certainly never missed one at the Methodist Church. A lifelong member of the church, he reportedly had not missed a service in decades. Frank Tully was the Lou Gehrig of the DeGraff Methodist Church, our homegrown model of loyal perseverance.

During the famous blizzard of 1950, a freak snowstorm blanketed and paralyzed most of Ohio. No one ventured outside for days. Roads in and around DeGraff were impassible, and all of the town's sidewalks were blocked with several feet of snow. Bob VanBuskirk missed his daily route delivering Hopewell Dairy milk around DeGraff, house to house, for four consecutive days. Kenny Fuson's IGA ran out of food because his suppliers from Columbus were unable to access their warehouses. Even the rural mail went undelivered despite the weathered creed of the post office and its noble carriers.

Frank Tully, DeGraff's hamburger-eating confirmed bachelor, lived on Cretcher Street several blocks from the Methodist Church, and each Sunday he'd walk briskly to church. There would be no need for him to walk to church the Sunday of the great blizzard because, for the first time in church history, the service was canceled. The minister at the time was Reverend Howard Householder, a man of good humor, who posted these words on the church marquee by the front entrance:

Church Canceled This Sunday. Hell Froze Over.

But no one thought to inform Frank Tully of this fact, and he didn't see the posting until, fitted with a pair of snowshoes he hadn't worn since his winter walks to DeGraff School almost five decades past, he had trudged through several sidewalks and made his way to the church's front doors. I cannot begin to imagine Frank's combined surprise and disappointment at having journeyed to church in such impossible conditions only to discover the service was canceled. According to Reverend Householder's wife, Thelma, who was watching from a window in their home beside the church, mounds of snow scattered as Frank opened the church's massive oak doors and stepped inside.

Mrs. Householder told the Reverend about Frank, and together they watched for him to leave the church. When he emerged, they called out to him from their front door and invited him to come inside for a cup of coffee. According to Reverend Householder during his sermon the following Sunday of which Frank Tully was the topic, Frank smiled but turned down their invitation. "Sorry, Reverend and Mrs. Householder, but I've got a deep walk home. I enjoyed the sermon today, Reverend. Your best one in years!" Reverend Householder wasn't the only man of good humor in DeGraff.

During church services, Frank Tully always sat in the first pew directly in front of the pulpit. His distinctive, high-pitched voice stood out from the collective voices of the rest of the congregation, but even more so because his responses were invariably a word behind everyone else's. He was a word behind during the Apostle's Creed, the Lord's Prayer, the Words of Response, and every verse of every hymn. It was maddeningly distracting, and oftentimes I'd find myself following Frank's vocal lags instead of being led by the minister.

But because Frank Tully was so blessed sincere, no one ever faulted him or requested him to join in unison with the rest of us. Like the day of his snowshoed, singular sojourn to church to worship alone, Frank was out of step with the rest of DeGraff. Or maybe it was just the other way around. Maybe Frank Tully was the only one in step and the only one with the proper cadence and rhythm. Maybe all the rest of us were out of step and too fast by one word. I don't know. I do know that every church needs a Frank Tully.

115

Rick D. Niece, Ph.D.

Every church needs a person of conviction who sits down front and leads by following.

So it was no surprise to see Frank Tully in attendance at the Sunday school's elementary student performance of biblical parables, sitting in the middle of the front row.

But it was a surprise, a big surprise, when the head of Kurt's wooden mallet flew off in mid-swing, somersaulted through the air, and banged off Frank's bald head before landing at his feet. Frank was wounded and Kurt was pained, but Jeff and I were the ones in stitches.

After an awkward moment of suspended cobbling, Kurt stood up, bounded off the platform, and hurried out to Frank. While rubbing the growing red welt atop his smooth head, Frank reached down for the mallet top and put it in the pocket of his favorite—and only—plaid cardigan sweater. Frank must have thought he'd won himself a door prize or something because when Kurt stretched out his hand to Frank, palm up in silent request for the top of his prop, Frank happily shook Kurt's hand and thanked him.

Kurt stood bewildered until Mrs. Shawan, the director for the evening's entertainment, called for him to return to the stage. He stepped back onto the platform and began to cobble once again, this time with a headless stick, but he was not a good enough actor to conceal his lost zest and thespian enthusiasm. The scene was tough to watch, but Kurt was able to fake his way through the crafting of a sandal and even managed a halfhearted bow at the parable's conclusion.

We were walking back to our car when Wynn and John Kinnan, father and son partners in Kinnan's Hardware, approached us. John's daughter had been a stable maid in one of the scenes. Wynn and John never missed an opportunity to needle my father who was rather well-known around town for his ineptitude with tools. Anytime

Dad entered their store to buy hardware or to ask for handyman advice, he'd end up being the punch line to a Kinnan joke. Always the good sport, Dad was an even better foil.

"Hey, Lewie," John chuckled, "looks like Kurt's a chip off the old block the way he handled his mallet tonight." We all managed weak smiles, except for Kurt, who was trying to figure out if John was complimenting him or not.

Wynn never let his son have the last line. "No, John," Wynn cut in, "after seeing the knot on poor old Frank's shiny head, it looked more like a Kurt chip shot off the old block."

Even though Kurt didn't understand Wynn's golf analogy, he laughed along with the rest of us and seemed to feel better.

Apparently my father continued thinking about all the ribbing he'd taken because the following weekend, he decided to teach my little brother the art of carpentry. Dad the master builder and Kurt his apprentice. That was quite a concept. They decided to build Lady a doghouse, and the entire weekend was spent measuring, sawing, and hammering. After they finished their work, Kurt nailed a neatly printed sign—**LADY'S PALACE**—just above the "square-oval-triangular" opening to the doghouse. I never once saw Lady enter her palace, but I don't think that was my father's point anyway. The contorted kennel stood crookedly proud as a monument to his sense of humor.

Toward the end of the week, after word about the carpentry project spread, Wynn and John Kinnan stopped by our house to view the construction. As he looked at Lady's doghouse, John Kinnan was, for once, speechless.

After a slow, chin-scratching walk around it and careful inspection, Wynn looked at John and then toward my father before breaking the silence. "Well, Lewie, I'll give you credit for one thing. That sign is spelled perfect!"

CHAPTER FIFTEEN

CANVAS-CAPED PHOSPHORESCENT MAN

Danny Coonzy lived catty-corner from us, and Steve Houchin's house was one block over. The three of us were friends, even though Steve and Danny were exact opposites and Steve didn't like Danny very much. Steve was athletic, assured, and smart. After graduating from high school with a perfect 4.0 grade point average, he was awarded a scholarship to attend Ohio State University. Danny was chubby, vulnerable, and struggled in each grade to make it to the next. Life never offered him any scholarships. If it hadn't been for his grandparents, Danny would not have experienced a family at all. I liked Steve and Danny, but being friends with Danny took extra effort.

Danny Coonzy had a difficult home life. His parents were either together and unhappy or separated and unhappy. Danny learned well from them, and as a consequence, he was an equal mixture of sullen and moody, making him a challenging guy to be around. When we were kids, his parents moved to Hoboken, New Jersey, and left Danny to be raised by his grandparents, Dolph and Mamie Coonzy. Then, when he was in the sixth grade, his parents came back in the middle of the night and pirated him off to Hoboken to share their misery.

In the bifurcated world of Danny Coonzy, people were divided into two groups: those who were pot-lickers and those who were not.

If Danny was mad at you, you were a pot-licker. If Danny was in a bad mood, you were a pot-licker. His parents, for the record, were always pot-lickers. Steve Houchin and I were usually pot-lickers. Dolph was sometimes a pot-licker, but Mamie was never a pot-licker. Danny's world was pretty pot-licking defined.

Danny had an interesting phobia. While some people are afraid of snakes, spiders, crowded elevators, heights, leaving the house, germs, the number thirteen, black cats, and broken mirrors, Danny was afraid of fireflies. Every time my brother Jeff and I excitedly captured these lightning bug insects that glow in the dark by hand-cupping them into mayonnaise jars with punctured tin lids, Danny would stand protected inside the safety of his front porch screen door and yell at the top of his lungs that we were pot-lickers. Jeff and the lightning bugs didn't seem to mind, but it kind of hurt my feelings. Danny needed a friend, and not many other kids in DeGraff applied for the job. So I was pretty much it for him, pot-licker or not.

One summer day, Danny and I planned a campout for that evening within the dangers of the vast wilderness otherwise known as my backyard. We pitched a tent by throwing one of Dad's large paint tarps over Mom's backyard clothesline and then weighted down the imperfectly formed triangle with bricks along each side. If Daniel Boone had known about Mom's clothesline, Dad's canvas tarp, and Danny's and my comforts, his trek to founding Boonesborough wouldn't have been nearly so challenging. With thick blankets, soft pillows, and plenty of RC Cola and potato chips, Danny and I were hunkered down for our night in nature.

We tucked ourselves in with some help from my mom and his Granny Mamie, then sloshed down potato chips with gulps of RC while reading Superman and Batman comic books by flashlight. After both the batteries and we began to fade, we drifted off to peaceful sleep, the tarp's scent of turpentine and oil-based paint hardly bothering us.

In the middle of Danny's mini-snores and well into the deep of night (okay, it was only about 9:30 p.m.), my scoundrelly little brother sneaked into the tent and strategically filled it with fireflies he'd captured earlier in the evening. He knew Danny's phobia, and he knew he was being a bratty brother. Yes, he knew all of that, and that is why Jeff delighted in the treachery.

Poor Danny! He began wildly thwacking the fireflies. They burst and, when they did, they gilded his exposed body parts. Where Danny had bare skin, he had firefly squish. The more he swatted, the more the innocent fireflies smeared and glossed him head to foot. He finally cracked and scrambled out of our makeshift tent, tangling the tarp around him.

And there went Danny, our tent trailing him like a wedding train, a giant lightning bug himself glowing in the night and flitting across the street to the safety of his house while waking the neighborhood with his serial screams of "pot-lickers!" He'd been transformed into the newest supernumerary comic book action figure—Canvas-Caped Phosphorescent Man! Pot-licker Jeff, finishing Danny's bag of potato chips, thoroughly enjoyed the moment.

One early spring, Steve, Danny, and I decided to build a raft. We assigned ourselves seaworthy titles and Steve, who had designated himself as captain, assigned us our specific duties. I was first mate and navigator, while Danny was relegated to crew and head deck swabber. Danny was just happy to be welcomed aboard and, for once, didn't complain.

Down the hill from our house was the Bokenghelas, an almost creek named after the last of Ohio's Shawnee chiefs. Bokenghelas Creek was truly mild, but that didn't matter to me. I loved the creek and spent many hours wading in it, skipping flat stones on it, and fishing futilely in youthful bliss. But floating on a raft down the Bokenghelas? Now that was my ultimate dream.

The box factory manufactured cardboard boxes of all shapes and sizes and shipped their products nationwide on wooden skids. We salvaged and dismantled several old skids from the factory and banged out a splinter-infested, almost-flat raft and then strapped two inner tubes to the bottom. After nailing on an in-name-only rudder, we carried her proudly down to the Bokenghelas.

In honor of Danny's Granny Mamie, who frequently treated us to homemade brownies and ice cube tray Kool-Aid popsicles stabbed with toothpicks, we named our raft The Mame. Granny Mamie was proud of her namesake, and she whacked a bottle of RC Cola on her as a christening before our official launch. The bottle wouldn't break against the raft's soft wood no matter how hard she whacked, but none of us cared. We thought the ritual was a fitting tribute to our many anticipated journeys.

Granny Mamie packed peanut butter and jam sandwiches for us to enjoy on our maiden voyage. Because Tupperware was either not yet invented or hadn't made its way to DeGraff, the sandwiches were wrapped in waxed paper and transported in a Fuson's IGA grocery bag. We soon discovered that creek-soggy peanut butter and jam sandwiches are barely edible.

We were all a bit too euphoric about our maiden voyage. The creek was too shallow, the inner tubes too few, and the three of us too heavy. We launched, hit bottom, and sat wet and motionless while the water curled around us in taunting ripples. We ended right where we had started.

We shouldered the raft back to our storage shed for future adjustments never made, and she was soon forgotten among the many other dreams of young boys during a short spring and long Ohio summer. I suspect my creek still awaits the conquerors.

Danny's parents hauled him off to Hoboken the following year, and I didn't see him again until a couple of decades later when he attended a regional Kiwanis meeting in Kent, Ohio, and found my name in the local telephone book. He was a tool salesman for an outfit selling merchandise town to town out of panel trucks.

At dinner that evening, I heard Danny's post-DeGraff history. He'd been married and divorced three times and had children he'd lost contact with, although he did have a billfold full of baby pictures. During dinner, he referred to each ex-wife and a couple of Coonzy progeny as pot-lickers. I noticed his pot-licker adjectives had become more profane since childhood. Even though he bragged he'd finally met the perfect woman at an Atlantic City casino and was thinking of marrying again, he still seemed to be an equal mixture of sullen and moody. I forgot to ask if Hoboken had fireflies.

Thinking back on it, I'm glad Steve Houchin and I were friends with Danny. A guy needs at least two friends at some point during his pot-licking life.

A FIGMENT OF MY YOUTH

Below the hill
on which our house was throned,
in my hometown,
trickles a creek.
In my youth I fancied
the creek to be most remarkable
and filled with enchantment, excitement,
history, mystery, and life.
I often visualized bloody pirate ships
besieged in battle upon those waters,
or sneaking German submarines slithering below them.
I often imagined many famous explorers
using my creek for passage to their quests
and carrying back tantalizing tales
describing the great white waterway.
And I was certain that my creek,
on a permanent peregrination,
had gone far, seen much,
delighted many, and disappointed none.
It even housed crayfish,
gigantic creatures with gigantic claws,
for me to wade after
even though I privately hoped
never to catch one.
Yes, I fancied my creek
to be most remarkable
in my youth.

I returned to my creek
after years and miles had removed me.
So different now
though actually unchanged:
shallow—no more than two feet deep;
steady—coming from nowhere and returning soon;
silent—currents hardly even murmuring.

I caught a crayfish
in an old coffee can
and watched it
scamper frantically
round and round and round
until I let it go
unharmed.

CHAPTER SIXTEEN

CARNIVAL COMING TO TOWN!

My brother Jeff and his best friend Mike Bodenmiller were always in the middle of something. Unlike many of their adventures, however, this time they'd landed themselves something productive.

A man named Big Red, the manager and advance man for a traveling carnival headquartered in Sarasota, Florida, had arrived in DeGraff a couple of days before his troupe to check out our downtown for the carnival setup. While Big Red was walking up and down Main Street with a clipboard and sketching out locations for the various rides, booths, and tents, Jeff and Mike, always the curious pair, stopped him to ask what he was doing. After a quick explanation, Big Red hired them both on the spot to nail "Carnival Coming to Town" posters on every telephone pole in DeGraff. He gave each of them a dollar bill, and they strutted around like they had suddenly become Rockefellers.

Big Red furnished a box of two-penny nails, a claw hammer, and an armload of posters, and designated Jeff to be the hammerer and Mike to be the supplier. He said Jeff looked like he could handle a hammer, quite an honor for one of Lewie Niece's boys. Since Jeff eventually went into construction for his livelihood, Big Red turned out to be almost as prophetic as the Gypsy fortuneteller who traveled with the carnival and peered into my mother's future.

During the middle of the carnival's week-long run, my mother decided to have her fortune told. Mom was pretty excited when, inside a colorful tent propped up in front of the DeGraff Public Library, the Gypsy seer looked into her crystal ball (Mom said it looked like a big glass ornament from one of the posts on an old four-poster bed), seemed to go into a trance for several seconds, and then dramatically announced that Mom would soon be coming into a large inheritance. This philanthropic prophecy only cost my mother a mere fifty cents.

Two weeks later, in an act of coincidence or predestined fate—who really knows about these things—my mother's Uncle Ed died in Lima. A couple of days later, she received word he'd left her two hundred and fifty dollars. It didn't matter how anyone else quantified what the Gypsy meant when she predicted a large inheritance, two hundred and fifty dollars was a tidy sum for my mother, and she considered it to be huge. After her evening of good fortune, Mom became a "you *can* see into the future" convert, and now trusts fortune cookies for their prophetic messages.

The carnival caravan, packed into several large semi-truck trailers and pickup trucks, arrived in DeGraff early on a Saturday morning. An Airstream mobile home within the procession served as Big Red's home and the carnival's headquarters. He parked his rig near the alley running beside Andy Stayrook's Auto Sales. Andy was one of the first customers on my paper route, and so Big Red's path was about to cross with another one of Lewie Niece's boys.

When I delivered my papers on Saturday afternoon, Big Red was standing beside his Airstream barking orders at two little guys who didn't look much older than I was. They were trying to carry a large rope but making a mess of it. The long rope—the fat, thick kind used on boats and docks—was tangled and twisted. The two of them were having a time of it, thoroughly entwining themselves in the jumbled mess more than they were capturing it. I'd never seen a boa constrictor engulf its helpless victim, but I imagined it would look something like this. Big Red wasn't happy.

"What the hell is wrong with you two? Are you complete idiots? I don't know why I let your uncle talk me into hiring on either one of you in the first place. You both register a record high on the worthless meter!" Big Red stopped to take a breath, causing his face to inflate even bigger and become even redder.

"If we don't get this rig up and ready in time for opening tonight, I'm holding you two numbnuts responsible. And when we pull out, I swear to God I'll leave you both behind to rot in this hick burg. That'd teach you a lesson. How'd you like to be left behind here?"

The boys shook their heads nervously. Then, moving their feet faster than the tap dancers on Ted Mack's *The Original Amateur Hour*, they hoofed their way down the street toward the center of town, skipping rope in tandem every couple of steps. Big Red mumbled something unintelligible and walked back toward his trailer.

"Hey," I yelled before he opened the door, "this isn't a hick burg, this is DeGraff. And if you left them here, they wouldn't rot. People take care of one another here."

Big Red swiveled around, and he shot me a glare that made me stumble back a step, but I courageously regained my ground and even moved a couple of more feet in his direction. Who was this guy to bully little kids and insult DeGraff?

129

"And who might you be?" he asked, looking me up and down. I felt like I was being measured the way Marshal Matt Dillon measured the doomed gunslinger at the beginning of each *Gunsmoke* episode, but I wasn't afraid. Hometown loyalties run deeper than fear.

"My name is Rickie, and I live here. You hired my brother Jeff and his friend a couple of days ago to nail your posters around town."

Now those were words of pure desperation. I could have said a dozen different things to answer who I was, but I chose to mention Jeff's name to validate me. It seemed to work. The look on Big Red's face relaxed. Everyone liked Jeff and, by association, most people liked me.

"Sorry, fella, I didn't mean to disrespect your town. Me and the carnival are glad to be here. It's just that those two little runts mess up whatever assignment I give them. Carrying rope is the easiest thing to do around here, and they even screw that up. But what the hell, I suppose they'll learn soon enough."

As Big Red talked, I carefully measured him as he had measured me. The source of his name was obvious. His hair, face, thick neck, ears, hands, and arms were all some shade of red. Eric the Red would have been reduced to Eric the Pink beside this guy. He also looked weathered and aged beyond what I presumed to be his years. Carnival life probably does that to you, and I figured he started traveling when he was about the same age as the two young rope wranglers.

He noticed *The Bellefontaine Examiner* canvas bag stuffed with papers hanging over my shoulder.

"You deliver the local paper?"

"Yes, I do. This is *The Bellefontaine Examiner*, and the newspaper covers all of Logan County plus state, national, and international news." Cripes, I sounded like a promotional banner printed above the daily headlines.

"Got an extra copy?" he cut in, obviously not interested in *The Examiner's* range of coverage.

"Sure, it costs a nickel." I reached into my bag for the extra copy I carried for opportunities like this and handed it to him like some kind of peace offering. I didn't know why I cared for his approval, but I did. I guess I felt like I was representing the whole town at that moment and wanted Big Red to know DeGraff was a good place to live. We weren't just any burg.

"Tell you what, fella, give me the paper each day, and I'll pay you in full before we pull out. I like doing business with you. Deal?" He stuck out his beefy hand that engulfed mine as we shook. "My name's Big Red," he said proudly giving my hand a big squeeze. "Glad to meet you, fella."

"Yeah, I know your name. My brother told me about you, and like I said before, my name's Rickie."

As I was getting back on my bike, Big Red reaffirmed our deal. "Just leave the paper on the steps of this trailer. I live here. We got a deal, fella?"

"Sure, we've got a deal," I called back while pitching Andy Stayrook's paper perfectly on his small front porch.

Big Red made our deal sound official, kind of like he and "fella" were now business partners.

As I delivered the rest of my papers, I kept thinking about how lucky I was. I liked having a hometown and a family. I liked the notion of living in one place, eating Mom's cooking, sleeping in my own bed, and having a fully stocked drawer of clean underwear and socks for daily changes. The image of the two boys struggling with the rope stuck with me. I wondered if they were brothers, and if so what happened to their parents, and how did their uncle have the authority to give them to Big Red and the carnival?

Rick D. Niece, Ph.D.

Some of my friends, especially Paul Whitehead, often pined on about running away and joining a circus. Paul's dream was to be like the character Corky on *Circus Boy*, a Saturday morning TV show. Corky was a kid about our age played by Mickey Braddock who, in real life, grew up to be Mickey Dolenz of the group The Monkeys. Paul tried his best to talk Ned Heintz and me into jumping on a train by the box factory with him and finding a circus to join, but the idea never appealed to us. When we were in the sixth grade, Paul missed school for a week, and Ned and I figured he had run off to seek his circus fame. We later found out he'd had his tonsils removed.

After my encounter with Big Red and delivering the rest of my route, I rode my bike back through the center of downtown to check out the various booths and rides.

Everything was scheduled to open at 7:00 that evening. Main Street was blocked off from the Methodist Church to the north all the way to the railroad tracks on the south just past the Sinclair Gas Station. This was the first real carnival to hit DeGraff in years, and it was definitely the first one in my lifetime. I was excited.

I'd been saving extra money throughout the summer. I now had more than twenty dollars and planned to blow it all on rides, games, and junk food.

My girlfriend at the time was Joyce Hengsteler, a ninth grader, and I was justifiably proud to be dating an older woman. After all, I was an eighth-grade junior high student, and Joyce was in high school. I was the envy of my friends, at least as far as the guys were concerned. The girls in my class didn't seem too impressed.

Joyce was out of town with her parents during the first part of the carnival's run, so I planned on going stag. We agreed to go together later in the week, and she made me promise not to take any of the really fun rides without her, especially the Ferris wheel.

Everything looked almost in place as I pedaled up and down the sidewalks of Main Street and watched the roustabouts finishing their various jobs. I carefully eyed the food concessions and planned my supper before biking back home. My meal was going to be an Italian sausage sandwich with plenty of hot peppers and no onion, boardwalk French fries with vinegar, funnel cake sprinkled generously with powdered sugar, and a giant cup of fresh lemonade to wash everything down. Looking at the prices posted on the front of each food stand and doing the math in my head, I knew I could buy all the nourishment I craved for about $2.00. Like my dad, I was a bargain hunter.

I hurried home and counted the minutes until 7:00 p.m.

Mom and Dad decided it'd be nice for all of us to go to the carnival as a family. I was okay with the plan because, as long as my parents tagged along, Jeff and Kurt wouldn't be too much of a nuisance. Mom approved of my carnival junk food choices, and Dad paid for them. I hadn't brought much money with me, saving the real spending for my time with Joyce, so Dad's offer to treat was a nice surprise.

I'm a sucker for games of chance, and I think the fascination started with that first carnival in DeGraff. Carnival hucksters are smooth talkers who know how to egg you into spending hard-earned cash at their booths. Promises of "you can't lose" and "this is so easy your kid sister can do it" are hard to resist, especially if you're a guy who wants to look heroic in front of his girlfriend. No carny pitch was good enough to entice my dad, however, and he wouldn't let me spend a quarter on any of the temptations. Since I'd have time on my own to win my share of Kewpie dolls, stuffed animals, and big straw hats, I agreed.

The evening with my family was a good one, and

because we enjoyed watching Kurt have fun, even Jeff and I got along without any shenanigans between us. We rode the safe rides, and I kept my promise to Joyce by saving a couple of the more daring rides and the Ferris wheel for her.

Mom liked the merry-go-round, and we all went around with her and Dad three times. Dad even nabbed a brass ring, allowing Mom and him to ride a fourth time for free. I stood between Jeff and Kurt, holding their hands, and the three of us watched our parents climb onto the same large horse, Dad in front and Mom snuggling him from behind. Watching them ride double back on the merry-go-round was a magical moment. It's nice when your parents are in love and not afraid to show it.

I enjoyed that night at the carnival with my family. In a way, I'm glad Joyce was out of town. Had she been there, I might have missed seeing my parents on the merry-go-round together and Dad grabbing the brass ring. I often wonder how many other brass rings my father captured for my mother when none of us was around to see.

The carnival opened again the next day at 2:00 p.m., a nice arrangement since it was Sunday and families needed time for church and Sunday dinner. Steve Houchin and I decided to meet in front of the post office and hang out together. He was much more adventuresome than I, and we always had fun, with him usually taking the lead in determining what our fun would be. Because he was a cocky, well-built athlete, Steve was the kind of guy carnies try to rattle and goad into playing their games. A mouthy carny and cocky Steve getting crossways with one another would be interesting to watch. And in less than five minutes, those two combustibles sparked and flamed.

The first gaming booth we passed was one with three solid milk bottles stacked in a triangle, two on the bottom and one balanced on top. The object was simple—three throws for a quarter, knock down all three bottles, and win a prize. But there were a couple of catches, as there always are with carnival games. You had to knock down all three bottles with the first throw to win the big prize. Also, the bottles weren't regular milk bottles and looked weighted at the bottom. The balls were much softer than real softballs, more like big round pincushions, and their lack of heft was a definite disadvantage for the thrower.

Steve was one of our star pitchers in Little League, Pony League, and later in high school. DeGraff had a tradition of fastball hurlers, and Steve Houchin could bring the heat as fast as any of them. So when the milk-bottle carny spotted him and challenged, "Hey, muscles, I'll bet you throw like a girl," I knew the action was about to begin.

Steve smirked. "How much?"

"Twenty-five cents, my muscled friend. That's one round quarter or two dimes and a nickel or five nickels or even twenty-five pennies, however you choose to pay. I accept all legal U.S. tender."

Steve pulled a carefully folded one-dollar bill out of his front pants pocket and slapped it on the counter.

"Give me my change up front. After my first throw, that big gorilla hanging up there will be mine."

The prizes displayed around the booth were separated according to the thrower's success. Knocking down all three bottles with the first throw won a large stuffed animal. If a second ball was needed, the prizes dropped down a notch to smaller animals and kewpie dolls. Using the third ball caused the prize to nosedive to a trinket or Hawaiian lei, the loser's consolation.

Steve had his eye on the big gorilla grinning down at him from the stuffed menagerie. His girlfriend was Roberta Dickerson, and I could tell he had already envisioned the kiss he'd receive from Roberta when he handed her the menacing miniature King Kong. Steve was confident.

Unfortunately, confidence can turn its back and run rapidly from the premises. On Steve's first throw, ironically his best of the session, he smacked the bottom two bottles dead center and, although they wobbled enough to spill the bottle resting on top, they stubbornly remained standing. He managed to knock down the right one with his second throw, but missed the remaining bottle with his third half-hearted pitch. No prize for Steve, not even a trinket or a lei.

"Set 'em up again," Steve demanded.

"Gladly, muscles," said the carny, smoothly scooping Steve's quarter into the canvas money pouch wrapped around his waist.

His second turn was as futile as the first. After three mighty throws, one bottle remained standing. Again, not even a consolation prize. The third quarter produced the same dismal results. He got more desperate with each squandered quarter. Steve was rattled, and the carny agitator knew he had Steve's number and his coins.

After going through three dollars, with only two trinkets and a cheap lei to show for his work, Steve turned to me.

"Give me a dollar!" No please, no thank you. No way I was not going to hand one over. The look on Steve's face was one I'd seen only once before, and that was right after Jeremy Robinson from East Liberty drilled Steve's Little League fastball two hundred and fifty feet out of sight. Our three outfielders never found the ball, undoubtedly cowering somewhere within Lafe Funk's cornfield far beyond the baseball diamond. When I trotted in from second base to calm Steve down, he gave me that look for the first time, and I hurried right back to my position. Steve struck out the next five batters, and we won the game nine to one.

I gave Steve my money. But there was to be no such happy outcome for this encounter. My three dollars eventually went the way of Steve's three, and Mr. Gorilla continued to smile down on us. That was one dumb gorilla. Being propped up on Roberta Dickerson's bed would have been a much better fate than hanging around this portable gyp joint, but the big monkey didn't know any better, and his toothy grin remained fixed. We were broke.

Steve snarled, "Let's blow this place."

The carny sneered, "My pleasure, muscles."

I sniveled.

My day at the carnival was over, and I was out three dollars with no rides, no games, and no funnel cake. As we walked past the post office, Steve handed his fistful of cheap prizes to a couple of little girls coming into the carnival with their parents. At least they were happy.

We hiked down to the Bokenghelas Creek to skip rocks. Skipping flat rocks across the water was one of our favorite ways to relieve stress. Steve missed the water with his first two throws.

My parents decided I shouldn't hang around the carnival every day during its run. I protested a little, but since I lived under their roof and ate my daily meals for free, I acquiesced.

I'd chosen Saturday and Sunday, the first two days of the carnival, and the following Friday and Saturday, the last two, for my times to attend. But because Sunday with Steve was such a bust, my parents agreed to let me go back on

137

Monday. They were usually fair that way.

I went alone and saw several of my friends, but I kept to myself. Since the milk bottle fiasco, I didn't want to spend much money but still treated myself to funnel cake and cotton candy. I was finishing the cotton candy when I stopped by a large tent with a banner that read "Nature's Oddities." A barker caught me trying to peek inside the tent's open flap.

"Sonny, fifty cents lets you in to see something you'll never forget, something you never imagined. I promise you will be amazed and astounded."

"What will I see?" I was now curious, feeling in my pocket for two quarters.

"Inside this tent we have the smallest man in the world, and we have the fattest man in the world. Give me fifty cents, and you can watch them both for as long as you want."

I was hooked. But once inside I was disappointed. The fat man was sitting in a throne-like chair and talking to several people standing in front of him. A poster hanging prominently above his head displayed his picture and name, "Man Mountain Nelson." Someone in the crowd asked him to stand up and turn around. When he did, I looked at the guy in disbelief. Man Mountain Nelson wasn't much bigger than Wimpy Knight or Turkey Thompson, DeGraff's heftiest citizens, and I could see either of them for free. Fattest man in the world? Heck, he was barely the fattest man in DeGraff.

I turned around and on the other side of the tent was the smallest man. As advertised, he was small. I had to admit we had no one in DeGraff to equal his stature. He was the first little person I'd ever seen, and the name on his poster read, "Teenie Tiny Tim."

A ring of people were staring at him while he did his

trick which was walking in circles on broken glass scattered on the platform. After several steps on the glass, a kid who looked like one of the tangled rope duo from the Saturday setup dropped more bottles and broke them with quick whacks of a hammer. Teenie Tiny Tim then stomped on the new shards. Although the glass tramping seemed painless for him, his expression pained me. He glared at each one of us in the crowd while rhythmically jamming his stubby legs up and down on the glass. When he fixed his glare on me for what seemed like an unbearable minute, I felt ashamed.

After his broken glass performance, Tim walked over to a dark corner of the tent and sat on the ground. He lit a cigarette, then brushed small pieces of glass from his calloused feet. As he puffed in the shadows, the smoke surrounded his head and masked his face even more. Except for the slow movement of his hand to his mouth and away again, he stayed still. And as I watched him, I shared his humiliation. I'd had enough and left the tent.

The barker called out to me as I stomped by, "Hey, sonny, how'd you like the act?"

I turned and glared at him, for what I hoped was an unbearable minute, then hurried home.

I HOPE I'M NEVER UNGLAD

I rolled on the lawn yesterday.
I rolled and rolled and rolled.
When I finally stood,
I was itchy
and my face was red
and my clothes were stained with green.
But I didn't mind.

I'm glad it wasn't snow or mud,
that it was just an uncut lawn.
And I'm glad I was itchy and red and stained.
It's hard sometimes to be glad.
It's hard when you are looking for something
and you don't know where it is
or even what.

I'm glad there are lawns,
and I'm glad I like to roll on them.
I hope I never grow bored with it,
and I hope I'm never unglad.

CHAPTER SEVENTEEN

HOUSE OF MIRRORS

As I delivered the papers the following Monday afternoon, I was still reliving my carnival adventures and anticipating what was in store the next time. When I made my routine stop at Bernie's house, I found him stationed in his usual spot in the side yard. I'd already opened the paper to the comic section and was preparing to give Bernie his daily *Dick Tracy* when he interrupted me before I'd even started.

"Been to the carnival?"

"Yeah."

"Are you taking me?"

"I guess."

"When?"

"How about Friday?"

And that was that. Bernie and I had a date, and now all I had to do was break the news to Joyce. I had talked to her before about Bernie, and she seemed interested in meeting him, so I hoped she'd understand. I was going to joke with Bernie about how he'd be a third wheel but, after looking at him in his chair, I thought I'd better not. Heck, he was going to be an entire set!

When I explained the situation to Joyce, she was hesitant at first but warmed up to the idea with a little coaxing. After a few minutes, she even thought we'd enjoy ourselves. I suggested asking Steve and Roberta to join us, and Joyce agreed. The evening was shaping up to be a good one.

When I delivered the paper on Friday, Bernie was waiting in his side yard with a sweater doubled on his lap. Again, *Dick Tracy* had dropped from the top of his priority list.

"Well, Bernie, you look ready for the carnival," I said, motioning toward the sweater.

"Mom thought I might get cold. What time we going?" He was obviously excited.

"How about six?"

"Good, now finish your route!" He was grinning like he always did when something out of the ordinary was about to happen. I finished delivering the papers in record time and got back to Bernie's house a little after 5:30 p.m. He looked even more ready, and I noticed several neatly folded dollar bills in his shirt pocket.

"Bernie, looks like you've got enough money to buy the carnival. Let me hold it for you. Somebody might pick your pocket, and you wouldn't even notice." I slipped the money from his pocket with a sleight of hand but bumped his chin for comic effect.

Bernie tried to give me a tough guy look. "That's five bucks, you crook. My mom counted it for me. I'm trusting you with it." I opened my billfold and nestled his money inside with mine. Then we were off.

I knew this was going to be a big evening for Bernie. He'd never been to anything like a carnival, and I was prepared to help him with sensory overload. I also had no idea what to expect regarding exactly what he could or couldn't do. With Bernie, impossible things somehow turned possible. Nevertheless, the carnival was going to present serious limitations for someone with his condition. In those days, no one gave much thought to accommodating the disabled.

Bernie and I met Joyce by the railroad tracks on South Main in front of the big food concession tent. Joyce lived outside of town and, since I was still a few years shy of driving eligibility, her dad drove her into town for our dates. She was waiting for us and smiled when she saw me wheeling Bernie toward the tent. She and Bernie hit it off immediately.

When we went inside for something to eat, Steve whistled to get our attention. Roberta acknowledged Joyce and me and then went straight to Bernie to give him a quick hug. Bernie was having a great evening already with Roberta and Joyce fussing all over him, so Steve and I mocked being jealous. Bernie loved it.

Bernie never failed to fascinate me, and I enjoyed quietly studying him and his mannerisms. I am usually apprehensive in new situations, taking a while to relax and warm up to strangers. That wasn't the case with Bernie this evening. He immediately started to talk with the girls and to roll his head in a figure-eight pattern that was sometimes jerky, sometimes smooth. The head rolling was a common behavior when he got excited, and I suppose the movement looked odd to people who didn't know him. I was used to it, and Joyce and Roberta didn't seem distracted.

Although I had to interpret for Bernie, my interjections didn't embarrass him. His sentences were strings of both intelligible and unintelligible words. I'd supply the hard-to-figure-out words in a way that kept Bernie from missing a beat. He did have a good sense of humor and was truly on in front of Joyce and Roberta. I was proud to be his friend.

That evening, Bernie discovered funnel cake. Sitting in his wheelchair and looking like a throned Roman emperor being fed by two handmaidens, Bernie could barely chew fast enough to keep up with the pieces of sugar-sprinkled fried dough being offered by the graceful hands of Joyce and Roberta. By the time he'd finished, his mouth, cheeks, and chin were smudged white with powdered sugar.

"Hey, Bernie," I chided, "you look like your pal Flippo the Clown. You're a mess!" His attendants quickly began to wipe him clean. When Joyce licked her napkin and dabbed at his chin, Bernie almost swooned. Her gesture was probably the most sensuous act he'd ever experienced, and he feasted on it. I kidded Joyce later, but she didn't appreciate the insinuation. I quickly and wisely dropped the subject.

By the time we finished eating, it was almost 7:00 p.m., and Steve suggested we get moving. We went up and down each side of the carnival trying to decide what we wanted to do. As we walked, we each took a turn pushing Bernie, and he didn't seem like a fifth wheel at all. While he was one of us for the evening, that didn't mean our adventure was without its challenges. The first awkward moment came as we passed the milk bottle booth, and the carny immediately recognized Steve.

"Is that you, muscles? How about another chance at Mr. Gorilla?" He spotted Roberta on Steve's arm. "Bet your girl could use something soft to cuddle up with at night. What do you think, moon pie? Want muscles to win you something cuddly?"

I had to give Steve credit. He never said a word back to the jerk and didn't even look his way. Unfortunately, Roberta pulled away from him and walked over to the booth. She spotted the gorilla still smiling and hanging from the wire.

"Oh, Steve, look how cute that gorilla is. I wish you'd win him for me."

I came to Steve's rescue. "Naw, that cheap stuff is for

suckers. Let the suckers waste their money here. We've got better things to do."

Roberta seemed satisfied with my excuse, and Steve tossed me a thank you glance. Bernie, however, butted in with a comment about how cute the gorilla was and maybe we should take a chance. For once, I was glad I was in control and quickly wheeled him away.

Our second awkward moment came at the Ferris wheel. It was by far the most impressive Ferris wheel I'd ever seen. The magnificently massive revolving circle of lights and gleaming steel dominated the intersection at the center of DeGraff's downtown streets and towered over the Citizens Bank, the post office, Strayer's Department Store, and Morris Rexall Drugstore. Bernie looked up in envy. With no words spoken between us, Bernie and I both knew the Ferris wheel was an adventure beyond our reach. We could conquer Thatcherville Hill but not this gyro-mountain.

The five of us looked at one another, waiting for someone to make a decision and state the obvious. Steve finally broke the silence and suggested Roberta and Joyce ride with him while I stayed with Bernie. We agreed with silent nods of our heads, and the three of them climbed into a swinging car with Steve sitting in the middle. As they began their slow ascent, Bernie and I watched from below. The wheel gained speed, and they went round and round, waving each time they floated by.

"Looks like fun," said Bernie quietly. For the first time in my years of knowing him, Bernie Jones sounded defeated.

"Sure does, Bernie, sure does."

It did look like fun. I knew Joyce and I would eventually have our Ferris wheel ride. I also knew Bernie would never have his, no matter how much we wanted it to be otherwise.

While they were spinning around, my brain was also

circling and brooding about our carnival ride dilemma. Just before the three of them scrambled out of the car, jumped off the platform, and bounded down toward Bernie and me, I had a plan. Best of all, Mrs. Keenen was not around to challenge me on this one. The plan, I must admit, was pure genius!

"Hey, you guys," I blurted out as they hurried toward us, "remember the ride in front of Kinnan's Hardware, the one that looks like a bunch of giant teacups? That's a perfect ride for us to take Bernie on. That's a perfect ride!"

Joyce kissed me on one cheek while Roberta planted one on the other. Steve looked so pleased with my idea that I was afraid about his intentions and covered my mouth. He slapped me on the back.

"Let's go, Bernie," Steve announced while ushering Bernie through the crowd with the three of us parading close behind. "Let's go ride the mighty teacups!"

I don't remember what the ride was actually called, but each circular rig on the horizontally revolving platform did resemble a big cup. The ride looked fun, safe, and Bernie-proof—the exact combination we needed. Its mechanics were simple. The faster the speed of the platform, the more the individual cups swiveled around and around.

After we purchased our tickets and approached the platform with Bernie in tow, the ride operator looked hesitant, and I was afraid he was going to tell us Bernie couldn't get on. Steve didn't give him a chance.

"Hey, my good man, this guy has ridden every ride here, and this is the only one left for him to conquer. He decided he wanted to save the best for last." As Steve spun his line of bull, we began to unbuckle the wide leather strap keeping Bernie in his chair. Suddenly Bernie was free.

"Come on," Steve spun on, "let's get Bernie aboard before he decides this contraption is too slow for him."

Steve began to gather Bernie up from the right side, and I grabbed his left. As we gently lifted him, Bernie's eyes glided back and forth from me to Steve to me. He knew we were pulling a fast one and didn't want to give us away. This was something new for all of us, but we needed to act like we'd been performing our routine the whole evening. Bernie was doing his part by trying to look indifferent, but I knew Bernie. I could tell his poor little heart was probably racing like a go-kart.

As we lifted him up, I saw the now empty wheelchair and realized this was the first time I'd ever seen Bernie out of his chair. The chair looked small without him, and I was startled by the sight. The moment was an odd one for me, so I can hardly imagine how odd it must have been for Bernie. Being held aloft in a crowd of strangers, Bernie was trusting his friend and his friend's friend with his life. In that moment, he was completely vulnerable. Trust and friendship can go no deeper.

The man taking our tickets never had a chance to protest because we quickly swept Bernie into one of the big teacups and tightly squashed him into the middle of the four of us. The cup wasn't built for five, but we made it fit. As soon as the operator saw that we were loaded and ready, he pushed the lever full-throttle forward. We swung side to side to side, screaming and squealing and shrieking in laughter while, like an octopus, we held Bernie firmly in place with our combined eight hands. It was the ride of Bernie's life.

When we slowed to stop, Joyce yelled for the man to give us another ride and promised we'd pay after it was over. He slapped the lever forward, and again we tossed and turned and clung to Bernie for dear life.

After we finished the second time, we scooped Bernie out of the cup and returned him safely to his chair. He was quivering in ecstasy. Joyce buckled him in while Roberta, feeling the air begin to chill, guided his sweater over his wriggling arms and head. I reached for my billfold and started toward the ticket booth to pay for our second ride, but the operator waved me off. "That one's on me. Just don't tell Big Red." I thanked him and promised to keep our secret.

We spent the rest of the evening going booth to booth and ride to ride. Earlier in the evening, we had agreed not to leave Bernie alone, so sometimes Steve and Roberta would ride and other times Joyce and I had our turn. Bernie never asked to ride on anything else and seemed content to watch. It's nice when once of something is enough.

We saved the Fun House for last. I had gone through it earlier in the week to check out the features and make certain everything was safe and accessible for Bernie. The Fun House was actually just another big tent filled with things designed to scare little kids and entertain adults.

Our favorite part was "The House of Mirrors" in which a series of mirrors distorted human bodies and faces into hilariously grotesque shapes and sizes. Bernie loved it! We rolled him mirror to mirror and paused at each one so he could absorb the full comic effect. Steve, Roberta, and Joyce decided to stay for a while longer, while Bernie and I moved down to the next section of mirrors.

Mirrors were placed at various angles and heights, creating an unsettling illusion of multiplicity. Bernie and I were the only ones there. As we looked at our reflections, we were surrounded by dozens and dozens of images of our bodies. We each studied our repeated selves, the older boy in his wheelchair and the younger boy behind him. Bernie seemed to be seeing us—himself and me—for the first time. He broke my heart when he finally spoke.

"We really are different, aren't we, Rickie?"

148

He looked devastated. I might have been able to fool one Bernie, but at that moment all these multiple Bernies were too much for me to manage.

"We aren't that different, Bernie. You and I aren't that different. We really aren't."

My words sounded hollow. We were different. The reflections of truth staring back at us did not lie no matter how much I wanted them to.

When the evening ended, Steve and Roberta left for his house, and Joyce and I wheeled Bernie to her dad's car where he was waiting for us by the railroad tracks. I gave her a quick hug and opened the door, reminding her that the next night, the last Saturday of the carnival, would be just for us. She smiled and leaned down to kiss Bernie on the forehead. Her hand lingered on his shoulder for a few seconds before she kissed his forehead again. As I began to close the car door, Bernie summed up his night with a simple, "Thanks," speaking perfectly for both of us.

After I pushed Bernie home and was opening the porch door for him, I slipped the five dollars back into his front shirt pocket. The move was my best sleight of hand, and he barely noticed. I stepped back and began to walk away, but turned again to face Bernie who was still sitting in the doorway where I'd wheeled him. "Sorry about the Ferris wheel, buddy."

Bernie almost looked me in the eye. "Oh, that's okay." For once, he didn't sound convincing.

And for several months after, I wished I had done more.

As planned, the last evening of the carnival was for Joyce and me. We were finally together without family and friends. We rode all the rides, except the Ferris wheel, at least once and some two or three times. We decided to save the Ferris wheel for our last romantic ride. The carnival didn't have that many rides, so I had more than enough money left for junk food and a couple games of chance.

I had managed to avoid the milk bottle booth, but toward the end of the evening when we were meandering and I wasn't paying attention, we walked right up to it. The same smart aleck carny pitched me his taunts.

"Hey, little man, where's muscles this evening?" When he spied Joyce, he suddenly feigned suavity. "Ah, but I like what you traded him for. Nice taste, little man. Hey, apple dumpling, what can I do for you? Want to take a chance with me?"

I can fish all day and not have a fish take the bait as quickly as Joyce swallowed this guy's hook and line.

"Yes, I'd like that big gorilla up there. What do you think?" She looked right at me with those big brown eyes. "Can you win him for me?" My excuse for Steve had worked with Roberta, but I was out of luck with Joyce.

The mental image of Steve Houchin, a pure fire-balling pitcher extraordinaire turned into a flat-broke puddle of humiliation, laughingly danced in front of the stacked milk bottles. This was shaping up to be the rotten end of a beautiful evening.

"Can you win him for me?" Joyce repeated, her eyelids fluttering like hummingbirds. Being stuck between a rock and a hard place would have felt like a feather bed and down comforter compared to this vise grip.

"I can try, but don't get your hopes up," I whined lamely. "My arm kind of hurts today." Carny man shook his head and rolled his eyes like I was already a loser.

As I was reaching into my money pocket, mentally calculating how much this catastrophe was going to cost, a hand grabbed my shoulder and turned me around. It was Bill Haynes, my Little League baseball coach for three years. I had learned more about baseball from Bill Haynes than from any other coach. Bill flat out knew baseball. He asked Joyce to excuse us for a minute and pulled me aside.

"Rickie, I traveled with a carnival one summer after high school. I helped out in a booth pretty much like this one and watched people throw their money away because they went at it all wrong. Listen carefully to me, and I'll explain how you win." I always listened carefully to Coach Haynes, but this time I listened extra carefully.

"People make the mistake of throwing hard at the bottom two bottles and aiming right at the middle. That never works because the bottles are over-weighted from the middle down, and those soft balls aren't heavy enough to spill them." I was hanging on his every word now. "The secret is to hit the two bottom bottles high on the rims. The ball has to hit those rims. Do that and all three will fall."

Bill patted me on the butt like he did one of his pitchers after a conference at the mound. If what he said was true, I believed I could do it. My arm wasn't very strong, causing my throws to arch slightly, but my aim was accurate. I felt certain I could hit the rims' sweet spots.

I winked at Joyce as I flipped mouth man my quarter. He placed the three balls in front of me while pattering annoyingly, "I almost hate to take your money, little man, I almost hate to. But I will!"

My first throw was off the mark, hitting more of the right bottle's rim than the left's. The bottle on the right fell,

151

as did the bottle it was holding up, but the left bottle only wobbled.

"Maybe you'll get that bottle with the next throw," Joyce encouraged, but I was already into my pocket for another quarter.

"I'm paying for another first throw. The young lady wants the big gorilla and nothing smaller."

"Good enough. I've got all night," annoying man answered back, scraping my quarter across the counter and into his canvas pouch.

"But I'd like to use the same ball again." I liked how it felt in my hand and wanted to stick with it. He retrieved the ball and tossed it back at me with an exaggerated underhanded motion.

I took a deep breath, stretched my arm, focused on the bottom bottles' upper rims, and made my pitch. The ball arched exactly toward the spot I was aiming for and thudded against the triangle. Like duckpins faced with a perfect pocket hit, all three bottles gave up and fell down.

Joyce screamed.

Bill cheered.

I strutted.

Mouth man muted.

After our celebration, the carny reached up and unhooked the gorilla. He then tossed him over the counter at me.

"What's your name?" I asked. I thought I should know his name since we had done so much business together.

"Arnold," he answered.

"Well, Arnold, I'm Rickie, she's Joyce, and that guy is Bill."

Then, handing Joyce the gorilla, I delivered my exit line. "Tell you what, Joyce, I think we should name this big ape Arnold." We peacocked away.

As I turned around to give Arnold the Carny one last look, he was already hanging another stuffed gorilla on the vacated hook. He winked at me and pointed to a big box of gorillas. Even when you win, carnies don't lose.

The time was close to 10:00 p.m., the hour Joyce was to meet her dad, and so we headed to the Ferris wheel for our last ride. This was my first time to ride it, and I'd looked forward to the thrill all week. Only one other couple was on the wheel when the operator helped us into the car.

We started slowly then gained speed. I loved the sensation as we circled up and down, down and up while feeling the warmth of Joyce snuggled closely beside me. Some of life's best moments are the innocent ones and, if you're lucky enough, you realize how special they are before they pass. I was sorry that Bernie would never experience such a moment. But in his world of vicariousness, this was just one more episode he'd have to live through me. We all have a purpose.

After several revolutions, we slowed to a stop as our car reached the very top, and I looked down at the operator waving up to us. Everything was still and quiet. I could see my whole world encircling me. I saw all of DeGraff dressed up in nighttime lights—my hometown looked so big and yet so small. I, too, felt so big and yet also small. I could not imagine being anywhere else in the world. I was glad to call DeGraff my home.

In the distance, I saw the flat roofs of the box factory's buildings. The company had shut down for the evening so the second-shift workers could enjoy the carnival with their families. Bernie's house was faintly visible and cuddled near the factory complex, separated by the railroad tracks stitched between them. I knew Bernie was asleep somewhere within that small square block. I wondered if his body continued to twitch and contort when he was

153

safely tucked in bed. I wondered if life ever paused and quieted for him and his body. I wondered if he dreamed wheel-less dreams and longed for walking worlds in make-believe. I wondered …

Joyce nudged me back to her, breaking my trance. And then we kissed.

The whole town seemed empty the next morning when Dad drove us to church. The carnival had packed up and pulled out during the middle of the night. Big Red skipped out without paying me for his week of papers, the first time I'd ever been stiffed by a customer. P.T. Barnum was right, and I was the sucker for that day.

After church, I decided to walk home. In front of the post office, I found a ticket for one of the rides. I picked it up and saved it for Joyce's scrapbook.

The next summer, the same carnival came back to DeGraff. Jeff and Mike Bodenmiller again hammered signs around town and, during the setup day, I saw the two rope-wrangling boys. They now looked like official roustabouts as they carried a tamed, perfectly wound rope easily between them. Big Red parked his Airstream in the same spot by Stayrook's Auto Sales. As I pedaled my bike to deliver Andy's paper, Big Red saw me and called out, "Hey, fella, is that the local paper you're carrying?"

I was ready for him.

"Yes, Big Red, it is. It's the same paper you didn't pay me for last summer. Remember the deal we had? If you want a paper this week, I need to be paid in advance and also paid for last year. That will cost you sixty cents."

Although he turned an even darker crimson, I'm certain he didn't remember me at all. Who knows how many times Big Red had scammed little kids out of their paper money? I was just one paperboy in a ream of newspapers throughout his travelogue of small towns. He shook his head and laughed.

"You got me, fella, you got me dead to rights." He crammed his fat red hand into the front pocket of his overalls, waded around, pulled out a coin, and flipped it to me. It was a silver dollar.

"You carried my debt for a whole year. Will that cover it and the paper for this week?"

For some reason I bit the coin the same way I had seen Gabby Hayes do a dozen times in movie westerns. It tasted horrible, and I wondered what else Big Red had stashed away in his pockets. I wasn't even certain why I was biting the silver dollar, but I bit it a second time just for effect. No wonder Gabby was toothless!

"Yeah, Big Red, this will cover it. I like doing business with you."

Big Red smiled, then he turned and went into his trailer. I still have that silver dollar.

The carnival was just as much fun as the summer before, only this time I shared the rides with Marilyy Herndon. Joyce had decided she liked older men who could drive. Or maybe her dad just got tired of hauling her around. Who can figure women out?

On the first day of the carnival, I walked by the tent of "Nature's Oddities" and the same barker as before called out to me.

"Sonny, fifty cents lets you in to see something you'll never forget, something you never imagined. I promise you will be amazed and astounded."

"And what will I see that's so amazing?" I asked, already knowing the answer.

"You will see Pretzel Man who can twist his body into any shape, and you will see Lady Nellie, the fattest bearded woman in the world."

I was shocked. "What happened to Tim and Man Mountain Nelson?"

"Well, Teenie Tiny married a schoolmarm in Idaho and quit the show, and Man Mountain went on a diet, so Big Red fired him."

Curious, I paid the man and went inside the tent. Pretzel Man was a major disappointment. Charles Tamplin, who delivered newspapers with me, was more double-jointed than Pretzel Man.

And as I peered closely at Lady Nellie, she looked a whole lot like Man Mountain Nelson, only with a beard. I figured she might be Man Mountain's sister or maybe Man Mountain himself in disguise. Who knew? Although P.T. Barnum's words were again echoing through my head, I sure hated to think a carnival would intentionally swindle a kid.

CHAPTER EIGHTEEN

THE WARMTH OF A NEW MORNING

The two most uncertain periods in my life happened within months of one another. I graduated from high school in June, and in September I began school all over again as a freshman at Ohio State University. I was quiet at my high school graduation party and seemed to be the only one not having fun. My family had me pose for dozens of pictures in my red cap and gown. I felt like a butterfly ready to be released from its ruddy cocoon. Problem was, I wanted to be re-cocooned. I'd been successful in high school, and it seemed like everyone had big expectations for me as a college student. But I liked my life in DeGraff just the way it was.

Leaving my hometown would not be easy. Columbus was imposing, Ohio State immense, and I was assigned to a freshmen dormitory housing almost as many students as DeGraff had citizens. In DeGraff, I had a name. At Ohio State, by unsettling contrast, I'd be a fraction of a multiple-digit number.

I also had difficult good-byes to make. Not only was I leaving my hometown, I was letting go of my paper route and nine years of loyal customers. And I was abandoning Bernie.

Because I was his older brother, Jeff grudgingly accepted

my discarded hand-me-downs—clothes, shoes, school supplies, baseball gloves, and even once a despondent girlfriend. When I gave him my paper route, however, he finally appreciated something I had outgrown.

A Saturday in early September was to be my last official contact with my customers. The next day, I would be leaving for Ohio State. I figured after I told my customers good-bye when collecting for the paper, seeing them again later in the day would be difficult, so I asked Jeff to make the paper deliveries for Saturday afternoon, except for three special deliveries I wanted to make myself.

Since I didn't finish the collections until several hours past my normal time and late into the afternoon, I was glad I'd asked Jeff to deliver the papers. The stops at each house took longer than usual and each had a special significance. My first customer, Janet Hall, had a freshly baked apple dumpling for me, my usual Christmas treat, and she asked me to stay and enjoy it while we talked. She was a genuine listener, and I stayed with her for half an hour.

Andy Stayrook was a quiet man who seldom had much to say, but we talked for several minutes that day. He told me how he had planned to go to college but never made it out of DeGraff. Marriage, children, and work took priority. I asked if he had any regrets, and he answered he didn't. He emphasized he didn't want me to have any regrets either and made me promise I'd study hard and graduate.

Bernie wasn't in the side yard when I stopped to collect and that was unusual. His dad told me Bernie wasn't feeling well. When he paid me for the paper, Frank Jones gave me a twenty-five-cent tip. That, too, was unusual.

Miss Lizzie's money was under the front doormat, her regular hiding place when she didn't want to come to the door, so I didn't see her. Since she was on my special delivery list, I knew I'd see her later in the day.

Mrs. Hostetler apologized for not having any homemade cookies, but when I saw a plate covered with aluminum foil on the front porch table, I figured something was up. She handed me the plate and took a step back, smiling. When I removed the foil, I found ten fifty-cent pieces spread out like cookies. That got to me, and Mrs. Hostetler could see the emotion on my face. Emotional herself, she said college guys always needed extra spending money. She kissed me on the cheek and then turned to walk back to the front door. She stood there for a couple of seconds before waving and going inside.

The final bike ride up and down Thatcherville Hill was difficult. Since the day I had taken Bernie with me to collect, I felt especially close to my Thatcherville customers. Also, a couple of years before, Lady chased a squirrel across the road and ran right in front of a car traveling up the hill. The car hit Lady's backside and spun her around into another car driving downhill that also struck her. I was certain she'd been killed. But when I ran up to her, I could see her eyes were open, and she was still breathing.

Lula Taylor saw the accident from her front porch and called the local vet, Dr. Verbsky. In those wonderful days of house calls, he was there in less than five minutes. The two of us carefully lifted Lady onto the backseat of his car for her ride to the veterinary clinic. She spent a month there while Dr. Verbsky nursed her back to health. Lady had two broken hips and limped for the rest of her life, but she still followed me on the route, though slower and less fixated on squirrels.

Lady seemed to sense that this Saturday was her final time for the paper route. For reasons only a dog can explain, she never followed Jeff. I think it was because he couldn't whistle.

I collected a lot of gifts and encouragement that
Saturday. Fortunately, I had a wide-wire basket on the front
of my bike and a wide-open mind grateful for small-town
advice. Jake Long gave me a thesaurus from his days as
a student at Ohio State. Mrs. Frantz collected a small bag
of good luck buckeyes, and Mrs. Keenen put together a
cardboard box of first aid materials, "Since your mom will
not be around to take care of you." Bill Shoemaker handed
me a pocket compass because "Ohio State is so dadgum
big." My basket was overflowing.

But of all the gifts I received on my day of good-byes
and good wishes, none equaled the heartfelt practicality of
what Mrs. Harshbarger gave me. The Harshbargers lived
atop Harshbarger Hill, the steepest climb in DeGraff. Six
days a week standing upright and pumping hard, I pedaled
up that hill to deliver their paper. Mr. and Mrs. Harshbarger
were my only customers out that direction from town,
over half a mile both ways from the rest of my route, but
because they were such a sweet elderly couple, I didn't
mind. I made only one thin dime weekly for my efforts, but
the pay didn't matter. Because I was lucky to have a paper
route, I thought of it as my pro bono contribution to the
profession.

Mr. Harshbarger was stooped outside a storage shed
sharpening the blades on his lawnmower, an old-fashioned
push kind with a wide set of rotating circular blades.
Because he was a man well into his seventies who cut an
acre of grass weekly by pushing this truly self-propelled
lawnmower, I never complained about my bike rides up his
hill. His generation already thought my generation was soft,
and I didn't want to give him any further proof.

"Your lawn looks great, Mr. Harshbarger. This summer's
rains have kept you busy, but you always seem to be a step
ahead of the grass." He was a tall, lanky man who had

mastered the art of looking over his glasses at you while continuing to do whatever it was he was doing.

"Yep, I've got to keep ahead of it. Grass never sleeps, you know, except for the big winter nap. If this yard ever gets ahead of me, I'm a dead man. Mrs. Harshbarger would kill me."

I laughed. "But if she killed you, Mr. Harshbarger, she'd have to mow all this by herself!"

He chuckled back. "Please tell her that for me. I'm not certain she's considered the consequences."

Digging into his front pocket for change and then counting it out to me coin by coin, he again peered over his glasses. "Go on into the kitchen through the side porch door, young man. The missus has something for you."

When I reached the porch and opened the door, he shouted over to me, "And good luck in college."

Mrs. Harshbarger was sitting at the kitchen table, a cup of tea in front of her. The tea bag on the saucer looked almost dried out, and I had the feeling she'd been sitting for some time waiting for me. She probably had. The Harshbarger house was toward the end of my route, and I was running late.

"Good afternoon, Mrs. Harshbarger. How are you doing today?"

She smiled the kind of soft smile grandmothers worldwide have perfected and patented. "I'm just fine today, Rickie, just fine today. You're late."

"Yes, ma'am." I apologized even though I'd done nothing wrong. "Yes, ma'am, I am late today. This is my last day, you know."

Her soft eyes continued to look at me like she was seeing me for the first time. Or maybe she knew this might be the last.

"I have watched you mature over these past years. I

161

remember the day you started your route. You were such a little guy. Mr. Harshbarger was sure you wouldn't last, thought maybe our hill would make you quit delivering the paper." She continued to look kindly at me. "But I told Mr. Harshbarger you'd make it, that you would not quit on us. And I was right. Even now you aren't really quitting. You are simply setting this hill aside for bigger ones to climb."

I wanted to say something back to her, something meaningful, but I could tell she had more to say, more she'd been thinking about while waiting. "When Mr. Harshbarger and I were married, Mother wanted to give me a special gift, a useful gift just for me. Daddy gave us a pregnant sow. He knew the sow would be useful, and she was. You know, we had offspring of that sow every Easter and Christmas family dinner for almost fifty years. Isn't that a remarkable thing?"

I smiled and nodded.

"Mother wanted me to have something useful as well, something I'd appreciate every day. I think she also wanted me to have something to remind me of her every day." She paused, soft eyes still holding me. "You know what she gave me?"

I shook my head.

"Mother told me that when she was a little girl, she disliked getting out of bed early in the morning. She didn't like the early morning because the first thing she felt was the cold floor on her bare feet. 'Terrible way to start a day,' she'd always say. So her mother, my grandmother, taught Mother how to make a rug from rags. Mother made herself a small rug out of rags and laid the rug on the hardwood floor beside her bed. Every morning for the rest of her life, the rag rug was the first thing to touch Mother's feet."

Mrs. Harshbarger paused and softly nibbled her lower lip. "When Mr. Harshbarger and I married, Mother gave me

162

a rag rug she'd made herself. And every day of my married life, when I get out of bed, the first thing I feel is her rug against my feet."

I wanted to say something but remained silent.

"I've made something for you," she continued. "Wherever you go, wherever your life takes you, I want your feet to touch the warmth of a new morning, like my feet have for so many years. I am giving you the beginning of a warm day." She placed a sack on the table and slid it toward me.

I reached across the table and touched her soft, wrinkled cheek. It was warm. "Thank you, Mrs. Harshbarger," was all I could manage.

The rag rug Mrs. Harshbarger made for me was the first thing I unpacked at Ohio State. I unfurled it beside my bed on the dormitory's sterile and cold linoleum floor. And every day of my undergraduate life, no matter how cold it was, that rug was my warmth of a new morning.

CHAPTER NINETEEN

SOMETIMES GOOD-BYE DOES MEAN GOOD-BYE

After collecting from my customers for the final time, I biked home slowly with the bounty of gifts I'd received. I carried the gifts upstairs and spread them out on my bed to show my parents that evening. Then I went downstairs and waited on the front porch for Jeff to return from delivering the papers on his route. *His* route? I felt like a stranger in my own land.

As soon as Jeff turned his bike into our driveway, I hurried over to ask him for the newspapers I wanted to deliver myself. He handed me *The Bellefontaine Examiner* canvas bag with three folded papers inside. I looped the bag over my shoulder as I had done a couple of thousand times before and climbed aboard my bike for the last deliveries. I called to Lady who was lying in the grass beside our garage. She looked up, surprised to see me ready to ride again. Tail wagging, she arose gingerly, arthritic hips slowing her, but managed to prance closely behind as I pedaled down Mill Street and glided onto Race Street.

Race Street slopes slightly downhill, and I could coast

a good distance. On my right was Ernie's pasture field, meadow-green and dissected by the Bokenghelas Creek, with the bridge at the bottom of the hill. I caught a quick glimpse of the roof of our house and visualized Mom in the kitchen and Dad in his easy chair, heavy-eyed and pretending to read *The Examiner*. It's nice to know everything is in place even though you will soon be out of yours. I pedaled a couple of hundred more yards before turning onto Boggs Street to begin the first of my remaining deliveries.

Fern Burdette's house stood empty since her death several years before. After a nephew and his wife arrived from California to loot all they wanted of Fern's possessions, an auction was held to sell the rest. Everything sold but the house itself, and that surprised me because I thought her house was perfect. But people said it needed too much fixing and wasn't worth the repair expenses. Fern would have spit.

I parked my bike on the sidewalk and walked to the porch. Lady was already there curiously sniffing the corner of the porch where Fern's Duke had rested. Lady circled twice and then sat, paws crossed prayer-like. I watched her and figured she might understand our purpose.

I opened the screen door, unfolded the paper, and carefully rested it against the locked front door, headlines facing up and out. I remembered the words of Fern's first boss, the advice he'd given her when she was an apprentice journalist.

"Fern, never hide the news from your readers. Keep it right in front of them."

When I closed the screen door, the headlines were boldly visible just the way Fern liked them. As I got back onto my bike and called for Lady, I smiled and looked skyward.

I pedaled past the box factory and bounced over the

railroad tracks. Bernie was sitting in his side yard and watching my direction, but he seemed to be looking past me.

"Hey, Bernie," I yelled, "I'm stopping at Miss Lizzie's. You want me to wheel you over?" Still managing not to look at me, his head wobbled a no.

"Okay, buddy, I'll be right back."

When I stopped at Miss Lizzie's, I saw to my complete amazement that she was sitting on the porch, self-exiled from the safety of her house. Beside her chair were two neatly foil-wrapped pumpkin breads. I dismounted my bike and waved a hello, but I could see she was extremely uncomfortable.

"Great day to be outside, isn't it, Miss Lizzie?"

"I suppose," she answered unconvincingly.

Miss Lizzie looked out of place, even on the porch of the house that had been her home for more than half a century.

"I figured when I saw your little brother go by earlier, without leaving me my paper, that you might deliver it yourself. I was hoping you would."

Miss Lizzie leaned down and carefully lifted both loaves up and onto her lap.

"Your brother looks nice. Your parents are doing a good job raising you boys."

"Thanks, Miss Lizzie. Yeah, Jeff's okay, and he'll be a decent replacement. I think you'll like him."

As she stood, I noticed how sad she looked, and I felt sad with her. She handed me the treasured loaves, grazing my hand twice. Then very simply and very gently, she brushed her hand through my hair and whispered, "When you find your love, keep her. And, my friend, be safe. The world is a dangerous place. Please be safe." With that she scurried into her house and closed the door.

I carefully set the loaves in the basket and climbed onto

Rick D. Niece, Ph.D.

my bike, all the while looking back at Miss Lizzie's front door. I made a U-turn and coasted back to Bernie's, parking on the grass a few feet from him. He still wouldn't look at me, and I tried to ignore the discomfort for both of us.

"Bernie, are you feeling better? You weren't outside when I collected this morning. Your dad told me you weren't feeling so hot."

He answered but didn't perk up. "Yeah, I'm okay. I'm just tired."

Both of us fell silent, and Lady nuzzled at the foot of his chair. He tried to ignore her as well but couldn't resist her persistence.

Bernie finally broke the silence while looking down at Lady instead of up at me. "Think Lady will miss me?"

"Of course she will, Bernie, we'll both miss you."

I had dreaded this moment for months. Back in the early spring, I told Bernie about my plans for college and that I was passing the paper route down to my brother. I explained all of the reasons and answered all of his questions, but he didn't understand then either.

He'd been upset and so we didn't talk about it again. Regardless, the day we'd both avoided was finally here.

"Mom's going to help me with *Dick Tracy*," he said as flatly as he could manage, eyes still looking down at Lady. That was Bernie, out-of-the-blue Bernie.

"What?" I asked, knowing what he had said but asking anyway. "What did you say?"

"Mom's going to help me read *Dick Tracy*. She said she'd fold the paper for me." He was making his point.

"Bernie, I told you my brother Jeff will read *Dick Tracy* to you just like I always have. Jeff will read to you."

I watched him carefully, waiting for him to give me a sign, any sign of forgiving me for leaving. It never came. This time our silence was even longer and more

168

excruciating. Then Bernie, the one between us who had trouble speaking, broke the silence again.

"It won't be the same, Rickie. It won't be the same."

"I know, Bernie. I know it won't."

He finally looked up at me. And as I looked back at him, I knew I had made a terrible mistake the past several months. I had not been honest with Bernie, and I was the one person, maybe the only person, he could count on to be honest with him. I'd been acting like everything would remain the same for Bernie, like things wouldn't change at all. I figured I was the one changing, not him. I was the one whose whole life was turning topsy-turvy, inside out, and one-hundred-eighty degrees around. But I was wrong. I was not the only one changing. Bernie's life was also changing while remaining exactly the same.

For a fraction of a second as I looked into his eyes, I saw the world as Bernie saw it, and the view was crushing. His world was one long tunnel of waiting.

I placed the folded newspaper on his lap, leaned forward, and gently hugged his neck. I felt his arms trying to reach around me, but they couldn't manage it. It didn't matter. We both felt the hug.

"See you, Bernie."

"Promise?"

"Promise."

"See you, Rickie, my boy."

I put my hands on his shoulders and looked into his eyes one more time. Then I quickly turned, got on my bike, and rode away.

On the ride home I glanced again at the pasture I had treasured for so many years. Shadows from several trees, especially the trees by the creek, were stretching out and reaching up the hill toward our house. I hurried home, not wanting to be late and miss a minute with my family.

Rick D. Niece, Ph.D.

The next day, I left for college. After driving away from our house, I cruised around the school grounds a couple of times, headed downtown, circled back to see Bernie's house, rode up and down Thatcherville Hill, went back downtown, and then drove through Greenwood Cemetery before finally passing beyond the city limits sign. I was satisfied I had seen it all.

The following year, my dad was offered a teaching position at Kent State University, and so my family moved to Kent, Ohio. I did return to DeGraff for a few class reunions, weddings, and funerals. Each time I went back, however, I felt more like my hometown's friend and less like its relative.

Looking back now, I feel certain somehow that I must have realized I was formally leaving DeGraff behind the day I said my good-byes and left for college. In the way people said their good-byes back to me, I should have known it was official.

Small towns are used to watching their children spread their wings and leave the nest. Sometimes good-bye does mean good-bye.

170

AND I WAS GONE

I saw myself

in your eyes,

and I was sorry

because you looked

so lonely.

But then you blinked

and I was gone.

CHAPTER TWENTY

PROMISES

Soon after we were married, Sherée asked me to make two promises. First, she made me promise I would take her to DeGraff. Because I talked so much about my hometown and my friends, she felt she already knew most of them and deserved to be formally introduced. Her second request was more challenging. Afraid I would begin to forget the stories I repeated so often, she made me promise to write about life in DeGraff. I promised to do both.

I'd also made a promise to an old friend many years ago. I had promised Bernie Jones I would see him again. Technically, but only technically, I'd kept that promise. I did see Bernie once again after the day I delivered his paper for the last time.

Over Christmas break of my freshman year at Ohio State, Mrs. Webb, the Methodist minister's wife, gathered several of us to go caroling one snowflaked evening a few days before Christmas. We sang around town, stopping primarily at the homes of elderly Methodist Church members. When we caroled for Skinner Hittepole's grandmother, we were only a few blocks from Bernie's house. I asked if we could go to Bernie's and sing for him. Walking down Boggs Street instead of riding my bike felt strange.

When we arrived at Bernie's and began to sing "Silent Night," the porch light came on and Mrs. Jones wheeled him through the front door. He spotted me immediately within the chorus (Bernie's ability to focus his eyes always amazed me), and he grinned his silly grin while flapping his arms and kicking his legs in the air. The way he mouthed "Rickie, my boy" over and over and over again brought tears to my eyes. After we finished "Silent Night" and before starting "The First Noel," I pulled away from the semicircle of singers and walked quickly to him.

I took one of his waving hands in mine and held it tightly against my thick coat. I felt awkward. I was ashamed for feeling that way and didn't know why I was so uncomfortable. Time and distance change many things, I guess. Even though I'd only been gone a few months, my life in DeGraff now seemed like someone else's from years ago. But Bernie didn't seem to notice. He never moved his eyes away from me.

I was wearing a red Santa Claus cap with a small bell attached to the bottom of the cone-shaped tassel hanging from the top. I removed the cap and placed it on Bernie's head. He liked that and laughed while my friends applauded. Leaning down, I wished Bernie a Merry Christmas and grabbed his hand again. He said something to me I couldn't understand, but I didn't ask him to repeat it.

Then I let him go.

His hand remained upright and writhing, outstretched toward me as I hurried back into the chorus. When we finished our caroling and began to walk away, I turned around. Bernie looked happy and sad at the same time. I felt only sadness.

I heard the bell on the Santa cap jangle in sporadic rhythms as we passed the box factory. I swear I could hear it still, an hour later, as I walked alone on Mill Street.

Six years later, after graduating from college and completing my second year of teaching, I returned to DeGraff to attend Skinner Hittepole's wedding. I drove to Bernie's house after the ceremony. I was stunned as I passed over the railroad tracks. His house was gone, replaced by an additional box factory parking lot that spread to within a few yards of Miss Lizzie's house.

I could not believe my eyes as I stared at the vast expanse of blacktop and tried to remember where Bernie sat in his side yard waiting patiently for me to deliver the paper and read *Dick Tracy*. Bernie and his house were gone, and I was angry for not keeping my promise.

I tentatively knocked on Miss Lizzie's door. Although I heard someone moving about inside and thought I saw the slight movement of a front window curtain, she didn't answer. I only knocked once.

I then drove to Taylor's Restaurant, figuring someone there might be able to tell me about Bernie. Sam Hamsher, now using a cane and looking much older than I remembered, outlined the sketchy details. Bernie's parents had both died a couple of years before, and he'd been taken in by a relative of his mother's living somewhere in northwestern Ohio. That's all Sam knew. No one in Taylor's Restaurant or the post office or Kinnan's Hardware could tell me anything more, not even the relative's name or the city they lived in. And that was it for Bernie and me.

Over the years, I heard nothing more about Bernie Jones until the night my mother called to tell me Jinny Knief had located him. He was living in a nursing home in Lakeview. My pilgrimage back to Ohio now had even

Rick D. Niece, Ph.D.

more meaning. True, I was going home to celebrate my cousin's wedding, but I was also going home to keep a promise.

CHAPTER TWENTY-ONE

A PROMISE
FINALLY KEPT

My cousin's wedding was perfect. Coming home after years of separation from relatives with whom you grew up is nostalgia in its purest form. Conversations never lag because each story, embellished by time, is better than the one before it. I loved being with my family, and I cherished the echoes of reminiscence.

After a big Sunday morning meal (my Aunt Sally is famous for her cornucopian breakfasts), I began my journey to the Heartland Nursing Home. Heartland, coincidentally, was the same nursing home my Granddad Niece had been admitted to many years earlier. Granddad was admitted for only three hours before he called my dad and demanded to be taken home. Dad complied with his wishes and canceled the paperwork admitting his father. I'm fairly certain my grandfather remains the least tenured resident in Heartland Nursing Home history.

Granddad Niece had terminal cancer. I can fully understand why he did not want to die in a strange bed in a strange place surrounded by strangers. He wanted to die in the comfort and familiarity of his own home. And, five days later, he did. I've come to realize the terminally ill usually know what is best for them, while the rest of us spend those precious remaining hours guessing around it.

Rick D. Niece, Ph.D.

As I drove to the nursing home, my thoughts were about Bernie. To be honest, I'm not sure what I was feeling. It was a cocktail mix of nervousness, anxiety, and curiosity, all with a twist of panic. I wondered what I was doing, why I hadn't done it sooner, and how I would react when I saw Bernie. As I got closer to Lakeview, I tried my best not to think at all. But all I did *was* think and, consequently, I didn't know what I was feeling.

After I pulled into the paved lot at Heartland, I sat in the car to gather my scattered thoughts before going inside. As I looked through the car window, I watched three men in wheelchairs, two on the front porch and one in the side lawn. I squinted, trying to get a better look at them. For all I knew, any one of them could have been Bernie, especially the one in the side yard. When I got out of the car and walked past them, I made a point of greeting each one personally. They were friendly and pleased to be acknowledged, but none was Bernie. I was sure of that. They looked well cared for, and I felt certain they'd never be left outside in a thunderstorm.

I entered the front doors into the lobby area where a receptionist directed me to the nurses' station. The hallway to the station was narrowed by elderly residents, some in wheelchairs, others on four-legged walkers, and a few leaning crookedly against the wall. Intravenous apparatuses, institutional gowns and slippers, and portable oxygen tanks were everywhere. As I inched by, I tried to smile at the residents, not merely out of a sense of friendliness but to peruse them carefully. I wanted to see if I could detect a semblance of the Bernie Jones I used to know. Although their faces peered back with shades of hopeful recognition, Bernie was not among them.

The nurses' station was at the end of the hallway and served as a check-in point for visitors and a way station for patients shuffling between rooms. There, another chorus of curious faces greeted me. I asked one of the nurses about Bernie, and she said he was in room 102 and pointed around the corner. As I turned down that corridor, I saw 102 on a slightly opened door. Bernie's name was below the number. Sucking down a deep breath, I took several nervous steps forward and once again crossed the threshold into Bernie's world.

Bernie was lying on the bed, his arms and legs still jerking uncontrollably, although not as dramatically as I thought I remembered from years ago. His wheelchair sat empty in a corner. I had seen him out of his chair only once before, when Steve Houchin and I lifted him onto the carnival ride, but I had never seen him prone. He was watching a NASCAR race on a small color television sitting on a clothes dresser pressed against the wall in front of him. He hadn't noticed me come into his room. That gave me a few more seconds to glance around.

Several NASCAR posters hung on the walls. Most, I noticed, were of driver Jeff Gordon and his brightly colored #24 DuPont race car. The room was small but tidy. Bernie's head yanked toward his visitor and our eyes met, and I saw an uncertain recognition on his face. I moved toward him.

"Hey, Bernie, it's Rick Niece, your paperboy from DeGraff." I quickly rephrased my greeting. "Bernie, it's Rickie Niece."

Each time I think back to that moment, the instant he recognized me and knew for certain who I was, I feel a groundswell of uninhibited emotion. His was an instantaneous expression of shock and delight like I'd never seen before.

"Rickie?"

"Rickie, my boy?"

"Rickie, my boy!"

I tried to hug him, but we couldn't manage a real hug. I felt his arms struggle for my back. And that, once again, was enough.

"So, Bernie, are the nurses around here as pretty as Sparkle Plenty or Rita?"

Bernie laughed, and I immediately noticed he didn't have any teeth. I had prepared myself for how his crusty, yellowed teeth would look all these years later, but I hadn't prepared myself for Bernie having only bare, shiny gums for his smile. His hair was cut short and brushed up, and I stroked the top of his head.

"Bernie Jones, is that a ..." I said, pausing for dramatic effect, "... is that a flattop you're sporting? I thought we hated Flattop Jr."

Another throaty laugh emerged from Bernie. "Nope, no flattop, just a buzz."

A nurse came into the room and muted the television while leaving the video on. She asked if we were okay, and I told her we were terrific.

"So, Bernie, you like NASCAR?"

"Oh, yeah."

Looking at his posters, I smiled and gave a thumbs-up. "I take it you like number twenty-four."

"Oh, yeah."

I told Bernie that Sherée and I had recently gone to a NASCAR race in Daytona. I'd never been a fan of NASCAR before meeting Sherée and didn't fully comprehend the concept of grown men driving around in circles. But I married into a family of big fans—especially Sherée and her dad—and was now a fan myself. I told Bernie that Sherée's favorite driver was also Jeff Gordon. When he heard that, he flashed another shiny-gummed grin.

"How much are tickets?" he asked.

When I told him our tickets were $150 apiece, Bernie's

eyes got as round as hubcaps. He uttered a "Wow!" that had to have been at least five syllables long. Looking at him lying there in his sparsely furnished room, I was suddenly embarrassed about the extravagance of $300 for a car race. I didn't dare mention the $8.00 hot dogs or $4.50 soft drinks.

We then began a real conversation, sharing memories we had both kept treasured and safely guarded over the intervening years. Bernie's speech and unique sentence rhythms hadn't improved. I struggled at first but eventually understood nearly all of what he was saying. I was proud of us both. Bernie asked where I lived, and I told him Arkansas. He questioned why I'd come back to Ohio, and I gave him the only reason that mattered.

"Bernie, you're the reason. You're the reason I came back home."

He was quiet for a moment, his eyes darting back and forth and up and down me as he looked at me. After all these years, his eyes were still the only muscles he could fully control, and at that moment his control was masterful.

"You came to see me?"

"I sure did, Bernie. I sure did."

Later, when I talked to the nursing home administrator, I learned why Bernie was so grateful for company. She told me he had few visitors. Besides an occasional visit from a couple of relatives, his only regular visitor was a social worker from Bellefontaine, and her stay was clinically routine. She also explained that Bernie had become very difficult to handle, earning himself quite an unfavorable reputation among several nursing homes throughout the region. When something or someone upset him—and she warned me that he was easily upset—he'd demand, under no uncertain terms, to be checked out and placed somewhere else. As a result, Bernie had been through a number of institutions, but Heartland seemed to be working out for now. It was his second time around for Heartland. She assured me that Bernie and the nurses at Heartland were finally growing tolerant of one another. That made me feel better about his situation.

The longer Bernie and I talked, the more comfortable we became, and the memories flowed faster and more easily. Each time I brought up a topic like the carnival or Thatcherville Hill or our game of horseshoes, he'd light up like a birthday cake, roll his eyes, and "figure eight" his head in excitement.

At one point after the conversation slowed down and quiet eased its way back into the room, Bernie looked pensive. I saw him studying me in silence. "What is it, buddy?" I asked. "What are you thinking about?"

After a long pause, he replied, "You didn't forget me."

I fought back tears and stroked his buzzed head again. "Of course not, Bernie. I never forgot about you. I never forgot about you."

I'd wanted to ask this next question since entering his room and seeing him lying there.

"So, Bernie, the truth. How have you been, really?"

"Drifting," he answered without hesitation.

"What do you mean?"

"Drifting." His voice had a timbre that resonated deeply from within him before burrowing into me.

I looked at him closely. It's funny in a way, but that was when I saw the beyond-middle-age Bernie Jones, the no-immediate-family-and-few visitors Bernie Jones, the difficult-and-hard-to-handle Bernie Jones. I saw the never-to-be-forgotten Bernie Jones of a childhood long past and a promise finally kept. I truly saw Bernie Jones.

As I watched him, I noticed a single leaf on a barren tree outside his window, a leaf much like the one in O'Henry's short story. This leaf finally lets go. I imagine it falling gently down into the languid waters of a creek and drifting slowly until being trapped by debris under a single-lane bridge. That was the drifting and entrapment I imagined Bernie Jones had endured and was continuing to endure.

At 5:00 p.m., a nurse named Lisa brought Bernie his supper. We'd been together since early afternoon, and I felt I should leave them alone while he ate. I asked about visitors' hours, and the nurse explained that visitors were permitted until 7:00 p.m., but since I had traveled so far, they could make an exception. I told Bernie I was going to leave for a while and asked if he needed anything.

"A puppy."

"What?"

"A puppy soft like Lady."

"Now, Bernie, you know you cannot have a pet," Nurse Lisa announced as much to me as to Bernie. I think she suspected I was going to go out and buy him a puppy (she actually read me pretty well!). "You know pets are not allowed."

"Phooey," Bernie huffed. That was the first time during the visit I saw the agitated side of him. "Phooey," he repeated again just in case we had somehow missed his displeasure the first time. And then, for good measure, a third, "Phooey." He was making his point to both of us, but a kennel full of phooey was not going to produce a puppy.

I winked at Bernie and told him I'd be back in an hour.

"Promise?"

"Promise."

I stopped at the nurses' station to ask about Bernie's health and why he was in bed. A nurse told me that Bernie was permitted to be in his wheelchair for only one hour a day. He had developed a chronic spinal condition over the years and, as a result, was now mostly bedridden. She said he needed to be as flat as possible. He'd also been diagnosed with a heart ailment that meant he should not exert himself. As a result, Bernie was confined to bed for twenty-three hours of every day.

I could not imagine Bernie without his wheelchair. The chair had been a companion his entire life, but now it sat empty except for one hour a day. When I was a kid, I felt sorry for him being in a wheelchair. As it turned out, the wheelchair years may have been his best years. How ironic is that?

I drove to Bellefontaine, the nearest location for a Wal-Mart. I had a twofold mission: to find something with Jeff Gordon's picture on it and to search the stuffed animal section for a soft and cuddly puppy. I had success. It was one of the few times I'd ever been able to locate items on my own in a Wal-Mart.

When I returned to Heartland about an hour later, the door to Bernie's room was closed. Hesitant to violate his privacy, I asked one of the nurses if I could go in, and she opened the door for me. The television was off and Bernie was awake, staring through the wall in front of him. I think he doubted I would return. Disappointments can pile up quickly when life is reduced to a bed in a small nursing home room.

"How was supper, Bernie?"

His head snapped toward me, face now grinning. "The same," he answered devilishly, "but always better when Lisa feeds me." We guys never change regardless of our age or condition.

His curiosity kicked in when he spotted the plastic Wal-Mart bag. He stared at it but didn't ask about the contents. I reached inside and pulled out a soft black-and-white puppy. She wasn't a Dalmatian like Lady, but the coloring was right. I set her beside Bernie's pillow.

"She isn't a real puppy, Bernie, but she's as good as I can do. I gave her a name if it's okay with you. What do you think about Second Lady?" He grinned his toothless grin.

I adjusted Second Lady closer to his face and then cuddled the softness against his cheek. Bernie also liked the plastic, one-quart insulated Jeff Gordon thirst quencher with a built-in straw I bought for him. Yes, he liked the mug, but he loved Second Lady. One of these days, hopefully, I'll learn that sentimentality trumps practicality every day of the week.

We reminisced until after 9:00 p.m. when the night nurse let me know I needed to leave. Neither Bernie nor I wanted our day to end.

"Bernie, this has been a day for my memory book. What about you?"

"Yeah."

"Listen, I won't be able to visit you again for a while, but I'll come back, I promise. You know I'm promising that, right?" I watched his face for approval. It took a while, but it finally came.

I rubbed his head once more and teased him by saying "Flattop," then walked away from his bed. As I reached the door, Bernie called out, "Good-bye, Rickie, my boy. Good-bye."

"Hey, Bernie, not good-bye. I'll see you again, I promise." He didn't say anything else.

I asked the night nurse if Bernie needed financial help, and she explained that all of his needs were being met. She also said that adjusting to nursing home life had been difficult for Bernie because he'd been raised in a real home with loving parents. She said he talked a lot about DeGraff and me. I wanted to believe her.

I walked back to look in on him once more. His door was opened slightly, but Bernie was already asleep with Second

Lady by his head. As he slept, his arms and legs continued to dance involuntarily. Now I finally knew. Bernie's body could not rest even at rest. As I watched him, I wished I knew more about why he was like he was and how it felt to have no control over your own body or your own life. In those moments, whatever complexities I thought my life contained disappeared. I watched him for several minutes until I felt I had seen enough.

I whistled during my drive back to Lima, something from Tchaikovsky and the Everly Brothers I think. During the return flight to Little Rock, I closed my eyes but couldn't sleep. I kept going over everything in my mind because I did not want to forget even the smallest detail. For the entire flight, I remembered everything all over again. And again.

Who knows why we remember what we remember? Forget what we forget? Keep what we keep?

I know why.

Remember Me

Remember me.

I have borne this life
with seldom tears
though often pained.
I rue those who live complaints.
My body, pretzel-shaped and salted,
bends stiffly
and threatens breaking.
My eyes are thick.
My gums are empty.
My head is smooth.
My legs have tripled.
I shuffle, wobble, teeter,
but seldom fall.
And as I look around me,
I see my semblances
shuffling, wobbling, teetering.
We mumble toward each other and nod.

At Christmas time
and Birthday time
we share each other's cards
and reminisce—
a son, a daughter,
now and then
a surprise great-grandchild.
Someone once
sent me a dozen oranges
and a pair of gray wool mittens.
Remember me.

CHAPTER TWENTY-TWO

MAX BERNARD JONES

Nine weeks after my visit with Bernie, I received a letter from Jinny Knief, our next-door neighbor in DeGraff. It was addressed in a neat cursive style seemingly beyond the capability of a woman Jinny's age. The thin envelope felt ominous, and I was hesitant to open it. So I didn't. I laid it aside until later, after everyone had gone for the day, and I was alone in my campus office. I had not received a letter from Jinny in years and now this? My hands trembled as I carefully slit open the envelope.

In all the years I've known Jinny Knief, she's never minced words, and this time was no exception as she cut straight to the point. Bernie had died. He'd suffered a heart attack and died two days later. Jinny explained she was sorry that no one had contacted me, but they did not realize the seriousness of his condition until it was too late. She wrote that Eunice Yoder attended the funeral and told her how peaceful Bernie looked in his casket.

Enclosed with her letter was an obituary clipped from *The Bellefontaine Examiner*. It was extremely brief, his name in bold capital letters:

MAX BERNARD JONES

I guess Bernie's life wasn't much to write about. Anyone reading the obituary might think he hardly had a life at all.

Rick D. Niece, Ph.D.

I would have gone to his funeral. Because Bernie's life and mine were out of sync for so many years, I suppose the timing of my finding out about the funeral after it had occurred was to be expected. My timing is usually better. I cannot speak for Bernie's.

Several things still haunt me today. The last time I saw Bernie, his final word to me was good-bye, and that struck me as odd even then. In all our years of friendship, I do not remember us ever saying good-bye to one another. We usually said "see you later" or "take it easy" or "good night." I am almost certain we never said good-bye. Even if he had no formal education and was confined to a wheelchair, Bernie Jones was always two steps ahead of me in how he anticipated things. I'm positive he sensed something the last time we were together.

I wish I had awakened him when I went back to his room. I don't know what more I might have said, but I wish I had awakened him nonetheless. I should not have allowed good-bye to be his last word to me.

I also wish I'd been at his funeral. Eunice Yoder said he looked peaceful. Bernie deserves to be at peace, and his spastic body deserves finally to be still. I think I deserve to have seen him that way. I think I deserved at least that much.

And I wish, these many years later, that Bernie and I could have ridden the Ferris wheel. That ride would have spun him through a lifetime of memories.

A WISHED FOR VIEWING

"It seems unfair that now you die."

It's not too bad,
Just kind of sad.
So please don't cry,
I said good-bye.

"And once at peace, how still you lie."

CHAPTER TWENTY-THREE

DISTANCE MEANS NOTHING

Four decades is a long wait between one almost hug and the last. I get mad at myself sometimes for taking so long to visit Bernie. Other times, I'm overwhelmingly relieved I saw him again before he died. The well-intended priorities of childhood often get misplaced during the journey through adulthood. Some of us, however, are fortunate enough—and eventually mature enough—to recover past priorities. It's a memory keeper's purpose to rediscover, to relive, and to retell, and then to help others in their rediscovering, reliving, and retelling. Those are nice gifts to share.

Funny, but I've never dreamed about Bernie. I still think about him though. I wonder what he really thought about me and what other friendships he might have developed over the years. I would like to think his truly memorable adventures were with me, but I'd be selfish to believe my paper route years were his best years.

I also wonder if Bernie learned anything from me. Did he miss me when I left? Did he feel I had somehow let him down? Did I, in fact, let him down? I wonder what went on in his life after I left DeGraff.

Bernie Jones influenced my life, and I am enormously

grateful for that. Having watched him live his life in a wheelchair—with his second-to-second spasms and contractions—helps me reduce to their proper level of insignificance the mundane inconveniences of my everyday life. Bernie showed me how to live life without complaining. Because of him, I am better able to see through people who complain without really living. Because of him, and thanks to him, I disregard all complainers.

Most of all, Bernie showed me that simple is best, that common triumphs over complex. I'll admit that I needed several years to finally learn that lesson, but I have learned it well.

When I knew him, Bernie's world was a wheelchair parked within a nondescript side yard. Toward the end, his world was a nondescript room in a nursing home. Bernie, however, lived a life of real consequence within the inconsequential and seemed to know, long before I did, that simple worlds come to us and become us if we let them. Even in his drifting, I am certain he never really left.

We spend our lifetimes searching through a world of ever-increasing complexity for a simplicity that is already waiting patiently and almost in sight. It is, after all, within the borders of our own side yards. The beauty of a rainbow is not from where it is. The beauty is where we are. Distance means nothing. The pot of gold waits, barely hidden, at our feet. Bernie Jones taught me that.

Yes, Bernie, my boy, between the two of us, you were the better teacher, the bigger influence. Thanks for being my side-yard superhero.

REMEMBERING WHERE
THE RAINBOW HAD BEEN

If I could borrow anything
for just one hour,
it would be the rainbow,
and I would promise to hold it
so very carefully.
I would reach out
and ask you to share it with me.
We would look at our rainbow
and talk,
and I could watch it
double
in your eyes.

Then,
after the rain,
and after our talk,
and after the rainbow
had faded from my hands,
I would still be able to reach out
and smile back at you,
remembering where the rainbow had been.

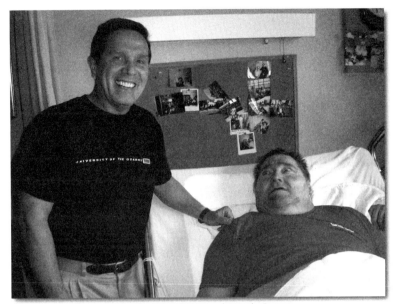

Rick "Rickie" Niece and Bernie Jones
Heartland Nursing Home

POSTSCRIPT

When my wife Sherée and I visited New York City recently, we encountered a man in a wheelchair and stopped to speak with him. He had cerebral palsy. I saw a tin cup containing a few coins duct taped to the arm of his wheelchair. We small-talked for a couple of minutes, but it was difficult to understand much of what he was saying. We did learn that he had been raised in Illinois but was now living in a shelter about a block away.

As Sherée and I thanked him for talking with us, I stuffed a hundred-dollar bill into his cup. Twice he looked down at the cup and then up at me. He was incredulous. "Why?" he asked.

I placed my hands on his shoulders and smiled at him. "That, my friend, is a long story."